D1168650

SAINT JOAN

Playing with Fire

TWAYNE'S MASTERWORK STUDIES

Robert Lecker, General Editor

SAINT JOAN

Playing with Fire

Arnold Silver

TWAYNE PUBLISHERS ♦ NEW YORK

Maxwell Macmillan Canada ♦ Toronto

Maxwell Macmillan International ♦ New York Oxford Singapore Sydney

Twayne's Masterwork Studies No. 111

Copyright © 1993 by Twayne Publishers

Twayne Publishers   Maxwell Macmillan Canada, Inc.
Macmillan Publishing Company   1200 Eglinton Avenue East
866 Third Avenue   Suite 200
New York, New York 10022   Don Mills, Ontario M3C 3N1

Library of Congress Cataloging-in-Publication Data
Silver, Arnold Jacques, 1927–
Saint Joan : playing with fire / Arnold Silver.
p.   cm. — (Twayne's masterwork studies ; no. 111)
Includes bibliographical references (p.) and index.
ISBN 0-8057-9436-0. — ISBN 0-8057-8578-7 (pbk.)
1. Shaw, Bernard, 1856–1950. Saint Joan. 2. Joan, of Arc, Saint,
1412–1431, in fiction, drama, poetry, etc. I. Title. II. Series.
PR5363.S33S55   1993
822'.912—dc20   93-13001
                                                                  CIP

The paper used in this publication meets the minimum requirements of
American National Standard for Information Sciences—Permanence of
Paper for Printed Library Materials, ANSI Z39.48-1984.

10 9 8 7 6 5 4 3 2 1 (alk. paper)

10 9 8 7 6 5 4 3 2 1 (pbk.: alk. paper)

Printed in the United States of America.

To Emily and Adam

Contents

Note on the References
and Acknowledgments

All citations of Bernard Shaw's *Saint Joan* are from volume 17 of *The Collected Works of Bernard Shaw*, Ayot St. Lawrence Edition (New York: William H. Wise, 1930). I have listed both scene and page number so that readers not using the Ayot St. Lawrence Edition will be able to locate quoted passages. References to the preface to *Saint Joan* are preceded by "P." Text passages from volume 10 of *The Collected Works, Man and Superman*, are cited in the text as *CW*, followed by volume and page number.

I am grateful to the Society of Authors on behalf of the Bernard Shaw Estate for permission to quote extensively from Shaw's writings, including the *Collected Letters*.

My wife, Glenise, lent me a sympathetic ear and made many helpful comments on the manuscript. I am also indebted to Professor Robert Lecker for his valuable criticism.

Joan and the Dauphin (Winifred Lenihan and Philip Leigh), world premiere, New York, 28 December 1923. Provided by the theater division of the New York Library from its Billy Rose Collection.

Chronology:
Bernard Shaw's Life and Works

1851   The Great Exhibition in London; 14 years into the reign of Queen Victoria, the glass-enclosed exhibition hall displays the products that gave Great Britain preeminence among industrial nations.

1852   George Carr Shaw of Dublin, a 38-year-old Protestant grain merchant, marries Lucinda Elizabeth Gurly, the 22-year-old daughter of a small landowner. On their honeymoon she tries to run away from her supposedly teetotal husband on discovering a wardrobe full of empty bottles. His dipsomania will turn his son George against drink for life.

1856   26 July: Birth of George Bernard Shaw, last of three children and brother to Lucinda (Lucy) Frances and Elinor Agnes.

1857   Formation of the Irish Republican Brotherhood (Fenians).

1867   George Vandaleur Lee, Mrs. Shaw's music teacher and a vigorous presence in Dublin musical life, invites the Shaws to live with him, thus establishing a ménage à trois that lasts until Lee departs for London in 1873, followed a fortnight later by Mrs. Shaw. Bernard Shaw later insists the ménage was totally innocent, yet he regards Lee as "an energetic genius" and is greatly influenced by him.

1871   Leaves school and serves as clerk in land agent's office.

1876	Leaves to join mother in London, and lives in her house for two decades.
1879–1883	Ghostwrites musical criticism for Lee and works for 1883 a short time with Edison Telephone Co. Writes five unsuccessful novels: *Immaturity*, *The Irrational Knot*, *Love Among the Artists*, *Cashel Byron's Profession*, and *An Unsocial Socialist*. All but the first are finally serialized in a socialist periodical. Educates himself at the British Museum, reading Marx, books on etiquette, and scores of Wagner's operas. Participates in debating and literary societies.
1883	Realizes the importance of economics when he hears American Henry George and reads *Progress and Poverty*. Nearly joins Hyndman's Marxist Social Democratic Federation.
1884	Joins Fabian Society and meets lifelong friend Sidney Webb, later a cabinet minister in Labour governments.
1885–1889	Book reviewer, art critic, and music critic in 1889 for various London periodicals.
1887	Queen Victoria's first jubilee.
1889	Edits and contributes two essays to *Fabian Essays in Socialism*.
1890–1894	Writes music criticism for the *Star*.
1891	*The Quintessence of Ibsenism.*
1892	*Widowers' Houses*, begun in 1884, is given two performances and receives mixed reviews.
1893	Founding of the Independent Labour Party. *The Philanderer*. *Mrs. Warren's Profession*. The latter play, dealing with prostitution, is banned and not shown until 1902.
1894	*Arms and the Man*, shown on a double bill with Yeats's *The Land of Heart's Desire*. Earns £829 in royalties. *Candida* (in part a satire on Yeats's play).
1895–1898	Drama critic for *Saturday Review*.

1896 *You Never Can Tell.* Meets future wife, Charlotte Payne Townshend, an Irish heiress one year his junior.

1897 *The Devil's Disciple* enjoys a successful run in New York, with royalties of over £3,000. Elected vestryman on St. Pancras Borough Council. Queen Victoria holds second jubilee.

1898 *Caesar and Cleopatra. The Perfect Wagnerite.* Marries Charlotte and after honeymoon lives in wife's flat in Adelphi Terrace. Publishes *Plays Pleasant and Unpleasant* in two volumes.

1899 *Captain Brassbound's Conversion.* Boer War begins.

1900 Writes *Fabianism and the Empire* (after Boer War splits Fabians) and accepts need for imperialism. Vatican makes formal proposal for canonization of Joan of Arc.

1901 Death of Queen Victoria; Edward VII accedes.

1902 End of Boer War.

1904–1907 Royal Court Theatre on Sloane Square, under management of Barker and Vedrenne, features Shaw plays, premiering *John Bull's Other Island* (1904), *Man and Superman* (1905, written 1901–1903), *Major Barbara* (1905), and *The Doctor's Dilemma* (1906). Command performance of first of these for Edward VII adds impetus to Shaw's reputation.

1906 Moves to country home of Ayot St. Lawrence.

1908 *Getting Married.*

1909 Beatification of Joan of Arc.

1910 *Misalliance.*

1911 *Fanny's First Play. Androcles and the Lion.*

1912 Writes *Pygmalion* for actress Mrs. Patrick (Stella) Campbell and begins platonic love affair with her.

1913 Writes Stella from Orléans that he has "been all over the Joan of Arc country . . . [and] shall do a Joan play some day." Death of mother. End of romance with Stella Campbell.

1914	1 August: Germany invades Belgium. 4 August: Britain declares war on Germany. Writes *Common Sense about the War*.
1916	Easter Rising in Ireland, suppressed in a week.
1916–1917	*Heartbreak House*.
1917	Russian Revolution in February. 6 April: United States enters war. Lenin and Bolsheviks in October coup end democracy.
1918	3 March: Russia withdraws from war. 11 November: War ends. Civil war in Ireland.
1920	Canonization in Rome of Saint Joan. First Meeting of League of Nations.
1921	Establishment of Irish Free State.
1922	*Back to Methuselah* premieres in New York.
1923	*Saint Joan* premieres in New York.
1924	First Labour government in Britain, led by former Fabian Ramsey MacDonald.
1925	Nobel Prize for literature. Accepts prize, requests that the money be used by Anglo-Swedish foundation to produce the plays of Strindberg. Mussolini becomes dictator of Italy.
1928	*The Intelligent Woman's Guide to Socialism and Capitalism*.
1929	*The Apple Cart*. Stock Market crash inaugurates worldwide depression.
1931	*Too True to Be Good*. Visit to USSR.
1932	Franklin Delano Roosevelt elected president of the United States.
1933	*On the Rocks*. Adolf Hitler appointed chancellor of Germany. Stalin begins vast purges in the Soviet Union. Visit to United States.

1934	*The Simpleton of the Unexpected Isles.* Visit to New Zealand.
1935	*The Millionairess.* Defends Italy's invasion of Abyssinia (Ethiopia).
1936	Spanish Civil War.
1938	*Geneva.* Hitler invades and annexes Austria. Neville Chamberlain signs Munich Pact with Hitler to bring "peace in our time."
1939	Hitler annexes Czechoslovakia. USSR signs non-aggression pact with Germany. 1 September: Hitler invades Poland. 3 September: Britain and France declare war on Germany.
1940	Trotsky assassinated in Mexico by Stalin's agent. Italy joins war against Britain and France.
1941	22 June: Hitler invades Russia. 7 December: Japan attacks Pearl Harbor. Germany and Italy declare war on the United States. 8 December: United States declares war on Japan, Germany, and Italy.
1943	Death of Charlotte Shaw.
1944	*Everybody's Political What What?* Allied landings in Normandy—D day.
1945	30 April: Hitler commits suicide. 8 May: Germany surrenders. Japan surrenders in August after atomic bombs fall on Hiroshima and Nagasaki.
1948	*Buoyant Billions.* Communist coup in Czechoslovakia.
1950	*Farfetched Fables.* 2 November: Dies at home. Cremated ashes of his wife and himself are scattered at the foot of the garden statue of Saint Joan.

LITERARY AND
HISTORICAL CONTEXT

1

Historical Context

Bernard Shaw had the good fortune to arrive in London at a time—1876—when the high Victorian noon had passed its apogee. Orthodoxies of thought, social behavior, and economic organization were being increasingly questioned. Darwinism, implicitly challenging Biblical accounts of creation, put Christian intellectuals on the defensive. Marxism did the same for defenders of capitalism. Shaw, in his early twenties, haunted debating societies in which, as he says, "there was complete freedom of discussion, political, religious, and sexual."[1] The tone was strongly individualistic, and women were encouraged to take an equal part in the debates. The gauche young man from Dublin had to force himself to speak in these political and literary groups, but early on he acquired the knack of holding an audience.

In the Fabian Society, established in 1883, Shaw found a home. Its advocacy of democratic, gradualist socialism appealed to young middle-class intellectuals who were dissatisfied with capitalism yet too realistic to believe in the possibility of revolution. Critical as they were of many aspects of English life, the Fabians shared the average Victorian's faith in progress, material betterment, and democracy. They held that socialism was but the next step in the evolutionary development of civilization. The work of the Society was vigorously educational; and through their tracts and their talented speakers, the Fabians came to have a profound influence on English political life, particularly when the Labour Party was founded in 1893. Sidney Webb, his wife, Beatrice, and Shaw were the dominant trio in the leadership, and Shaw was the Society's star speaker and one of its best pamphleteers. In 1889 the Society published *Fabian Essays in Socialism*, which Shaw edited and to which he contributed two of the eight essays. The thousand copies of the first edition were quickly sold, and several later editions sold out also, much to Shaw's gratified surprise. The volume was the first work to present "a comprehensive case for reformist socialism based on facts as much as ideology and written specifically for a contemporary audience."[2] In the wake of the book's success, the Society's membership doubled to 300, and provincial Fabian groups sprang up all across northern England. Shaw and other leaders of the Society spent much time traveling and lecturing to these outlying socialists.

Shaw was as radical a playwright as he was a social theorist. His hero was Ibsen, much reviled by the critics of the day as an obscene writer. Shaw came to his defense in the first book in English on the Norwegian dramatist, *The Quintessence of Ibsenism*. As a budding dramatist himself, he followed Ibsen's lead in writing thesis-laden plays dealing boldly and wittily with social conditions such as slums, prostitution, religious bigotry, discrimination against women, and medical malpractice. The plays generally received only small productions: as an avant-garde dramatist, Shaw did not achieve commercial success until the middle of his career, though one of his works, *The Devil's Disciple,* had a successful run in the United States in 1897–98.

It was with *Man and Superman*, written between 1901 and 1903, that Shaw surprised his politically advanced, secular-minded friends with a philosophical comedy that questioned democracy and had distinctly religious overtones. In this play and its preface Shaw put forward for the first time his philosophy of the "Life Force," which was subsequently to be elaborated on in several works. Shaw's view was loosely indebted to Lamarckian as opposed to Darwinian theories of evolution (which stressed biological will and purposiveness rather than chance mutations), and anticipated the more fully developed arguments of the philosopher Henri Bergson, whose *Creative Evolution* appeared in 1907. Shaw held that life is a force that uses human beings for purposes wider than their own, employing man's intellect to understand itself; the true joy of life, he went on, lies in yoking oneself to a superpersonal goal, to "being used for a purpose recognized by yourself as a mighty

4

one; . . . being a force of Nature instead of a feverish selfish little cold of ailments and grievances, complaining that the world will not devote itself to making you happy" (*CW*, 10:xxxiv). Great men and women, for Shaw, are agents of the Life Force, and he was later drawn to write about Joan of Arc because he regarded her as a devoted servant of that force; as he says in the preface to the play, she felt the "pressure upon her of the driving force that is behind evolution . . . the evolutionary appetite" (P, 14). This quasireligious position, emphasizing the superior individual's role in advancing civilization, weakened Shaw's Fabian commitment to democracy and would make him highly sympathetic in later years to dictators who seemingly got things done.

World War I was a traumatic experience for Shaw. By 1914 he had become England's leading playwright, the idol of thousands of young people and socialists. Almost overnight, however, he became one of the most hated men in England, attacked in newspapers and in Parliament, rejected by friends, and even forced out of the Dramatists' Club. The cause was a long pamphlet he published in November, three months after European hostilities had begun, entitled *Common Sense about the War*. Though it contained a great deal of superior sense, it also fiercely attacked Foreign Secretary Sir Edward Gray, termed English Junkerism as bad as the German variety, and misstated the causes of the war. The tone was all-knowing and often flippant. German propaganda agencies lost no time in publicizing those sections of Shaw's pamphlet most suitable for their purposes, and many people in England cursed the dramatist for rendering aid to the enemy, the prime minister privately voicing the opinion that he should be shot.[3] Shaw did not lessen the hostility when in the following year he publicly minimized the tragedy of the German submarine sinking of the passenger ship *Lusitania*. Undoubtedly Shaw drew on his still painful memories of ostracism and rejection when a few years after the war he portrayed the plight of Saint Joan, rejected by friends and allies, and hated by the English government.

The dramatist's depiction of Joan's agony in undergoing a trial for her beliefs may also have been to some extent wrung from remembered emotion of two other events in 1916, the trial of Roger Casement and the Easter rebellion in Dublin. Casement, a German agent trying to organize a revolt in his native Ireland, was captured and tried for treason. Shaw wrote a speech for him to deliver at the trial, claiming prisoner-of-war status, a speech that Shaw boasted would "bring down the house . . . [and] thunder down the ages."[4] The speech was read, but only after the jury had found Casement guilty, and he was duly hanged.

Also executed earlier that year were 12 leaders of the Easter Rising in Ireland and an innocent bystander and friend of Shaw's, Sheehy-Skeffington. Shaw wrote a protesting letter stating that the captured men were prisoners of war and it was entirely incorrect to slaughter them. He announced that as an Irishman himself he was "bound to contradict any implication that I can regard as a traitor any Irishman taken in a fight for Irish independence against the British Government, which was a fair fight in everything except the enormous odds my countrymen had to face."[5] Shaw's unhappiness over English behavior in Ireland began long before 1916, and lasted long afterward, but it reached a new height in that year, and it enabled him to sympathize easily with Joan's patriotic desire to drive the English soldiers out of her country and to infuse the play with an anti-English animus.

After the overthrow of Czar Nicholas II in 1917 and the subsequent coup that brought Lenin's Bolsheviks into power, Shaw came out wholeheartedly on Lenin's side, announcing in public that he himself was a communist and justifying Lenin's dictatorship and merciless methods for destroying all opposition. Many Fabians, and even eminent Marxists such as H. M. Hyndman, did not concur with Shaw's laudatory estimate of Lenin. We shall see later how this estimate bears upon the way Shaw tells Joan's story.

The buffetings Shaw received during the war, and the prolonged horrors of the war itself, darkened his view of humanity. In such plays as *Heartbreak House* (1917) and *Back to Methuselah* (1922), with their respective prefaces, one can notice a more somber tone in the humor and an intensified disillusionment with mankind. Shaw now trusts more and more to the rare outstanding individual for any furtherance of civilization, and he is not sure that even such individuals can do much. This of course is neither the mood nor the outlook that can easily produce the sorts of comedies Shaw had been writing throughout his career, but such a mood and outlook might be suitable for attempting his first tragedy. One can almost sense his relief at finding an appropriate subject to deal with as he begins to absorb himself at the end of 1922 in the actions of a rare individual, Joan of Arc, whose fate was tragic and yet in its way triumphant.

The play Shaw created was only his third full-length historical work, and the two other ones, *The Devil's Disciple* (1897), and *Caesar and Cleopatra* (1898), had been written more than two decades earlier. He had touched lightly on historical matters in *Androcles and the Lion* (1911), and a few of his one-act plays, but his primary concern from the outset of his career had been with contemporary issues. Joan's story thus presented particular challenges to him of writing in a form he had not much favored—the history play—and in the tragic vein, to which he had been temperamentally averse. It attests to his creative vitality, and perhaps to Joan's quickening power, that at the age of 67 he was able to complete the last, and some think the best, of his major plays.

2

The Importance of the Work

The French playwright and critic Robert de Flers greeted the first Paris production of *Saint Joan* with the following words:

> The English burned Joan of Arc and it is an Englishman who has just consecrated to her the most elevated and most tender work that has ever been written in her honour. It may be that this is her final miracle. It is true that the Englishman is an Irishman and that he is a genius. We are indebted to Bernard Shaw . . . for a simple and straightforward Joan who does not count syllables of her hexameters as she used to count her sheep, and who seeks neither pretty images nor pretentious metaphors, a Joan shorn of great verbal elegance and who is poor in speech as she is poor in her garments, but who is so rich in courage and faith; moreover, she is a Joan who never shows any signs, as we have seen in other works, all the more irritating for being worthy of her, of expecting to receive delegations of choirs in her honour and to take part with great enthusiasm in her own commemoration."[1]

He goes on to report that the play brings tears to the eyes of the audience each evening, and "it revives in our hearts the most admirable figure in our whole history which learning and piety, between them, were beginning to freeze over."

It is rare for a play by a foreign author to be the best one to celebrate a nation's hero, and it is even rarer for that play to enter into the repertory of theatrical companies of many lands. *Saint Joan*, however, has the status of a world classic, and it is one of the most distinguished contributions to twentieth-century theater.

Though no one but Shaw could have written the work, it is less a characteristic Shavian play than an example of his versatility, for Shaw wrote comedies and this one partakes of the tragic and is very moving. Nevertheless, *Saint Joan* does share the hallmark of his best works in that it is, among other things, a play of ideas. And the ideas in this work, as we shall see in a later chapter, have an enormous contemporary relevance, one that will continue as long as idealists come into conflict with their societies, and as long as societies must protect themselves from the presumptions of people who think they are acting in God's name. As Shaw rightly says in his preface, "the question raised by Joan's burning is a burning question still" (39).

The relevance of the play is in part a function of its complexity, for like most important dramas it is multifaceted. The simplicity of its structure and the clarity of each of its seven scenes cover a web of interrelated and sometimes conflicting ideas. Startling proof of this was provided in 1940, during World War II, when the Germans occupying France allowed the play to be produced because it contained strong anti-English sentiments, but the Parisians in the audience, thrilled by Joan's patriotic determination to chase a foreign occupying power from French soil, responded to the play in ways the Germans had not anticipated.[2] The considerably different interpretations that famous actresses have given to the leading role is perhaps further evidence of the richness of the work.

As a theatrical piece dealing with momentous events in the fifteenth century, Shaw's play has the obvious value of offering us some pages of history in a most palatable form. For every person who has read a book dealing with that century, there are probably thousands whose knowledge of Joan comes entirely from the Irish dramatist's play. Shaw tried to put the atmosphere and some prominent ideas of the time into his work, and he believed that any history student who saw his play would be able to pass an examination on the period dramatized. Though one may raise questions about the historicity of parts of the work, it is doubtless true that a substantial sense of the period can be obtained from the play. And Shaw has the singular knack of compelling us to see that people of the past were not especially different from ourselves, a recognition helping to illuminate both an earlier era and our own.

Saint Joan has probably been Shaw's most influential play. All later dramatists who have written works inspired by Joan—such as Bertolt Brecht, Jean Anouilh, and Maxwell Anderson—have clearly profited from studying Shaw's conception of the Maid. And beyond the particular subject, playwrights as diverse as T. S. Eliot and Jean Giraudoux have benefited from examining Shaw's distinctive manner of adapting historical events to the contemporary stage.

3

Critical Reception

The apprehension that many people felt in the first months of 1924 over Shaw's forthcoming play on Saint Joan was voiced on 26 March of that year by A. B. Walkley, veteran drama critic of the *Times*, the very day the London production was set to open. "We are to have tonight a play about Joan of Arc, and it is to be hoped it will not be disfigured by those blithe anachronisms and incongruities of treatment with which Mr. Bernard Shaw in his quasihistorical plays occasionally delights to criticize the present through the past." Shaw's reputation for flippant wit and irreverence made him seem ill suited to deal with the heroic martyr whom the Pope had elevated to sainthood just four years earlier. Walkley warned that "the usual sort of 'Shavian' pleasantry about this heroine would be unspeakably odious," and he hoped that his misgivings would prove to have done Shaw an injustice.

The next day he graciously ate his words. Though he had reservations about some aspects of the play, most notably the epilogue, he announced that Sybil Thorndike played the heroine's part quite beautifully and that Shaw had done justice to Joan: "the great figure of the story remains a lovely thing, lovely in simplicity, lovely in faith . . . we think the play one of Mr. Shaw's finest achievements" (Evans, 285–87).

Desmond MacCarthy, another distinguished critic, was even more enthusiastic, as his opening paragraph indicates:

> St Joan is a play of many and splendid merits. It is immensely serious and extremely entertaining; it is a magnificent effort of in-

tellectual energy and full of pathos and sympathy; it is long but it never flags; it is deep, and I am by no means sure that I have got, or that I am going to get, to the bottom of it. . . . We are lifted on waves of emotion to be dashed on thought. Only a languid mind could fail to find in it intellectual excitement, only a very protected sensibility could escape being touched and disturbed."[1]

MacCarthy ends his review, the first of three he devoted to the work, with the judgment that it is probably "the greatest of Shaw's plays."

Not all of the reviewers shared this degree of admiration for the work. James Agate, writing in the *Sunday Times*, offered a more measured appreciation, finding much to praise—the trial scene, for instance, was "masterly," the cathedral scene contained "great pathos"—and yet much to criticize—the length of the tent scene, the superfluousness of the epilogue.[2] And a few commentators were entirely negative. T. S. Eliot, never a Shaw fan, declared that the Irishman's "Joan of Arc is perhaps the greatest sacrilege of all Joans: for instead of the saint or the strumpet of the legends to which he objects, he has turned her into a great middle-class reformer." This was a judgment Eliot adhered to, for in 1926 he termed Shaw's play "one of the most superstitious of the effigies which have been erected to that remarkable woman" (Evans, 293–94).

These British comments were not actually the first ones the play received. Its world premiere had taken place in New York City three months earlier, on 28 December 1923. A year before, the Theatre Guild had sustained a loss of over $20,000 in premiering Shaw's previous play, *Back to Methuselah*, whose inordinate length had drawn complaints from the critics. Worried over a similar response to *Saint Joan*, which was running in rehearsals over three and a half hours and would therefore cause commuters to miss their late trains home, the Guild asked Shaw to make some deletions. He refused, cabling advice instead: "THE OLD OLD STORY BEGIN AT EIGHT OR RUN LATER TRAINS."[3] Since the Guild's control over train schedules was rather limited, they moved up the curtain time to eight o'clock, but even so, many of the opening night's criticisms centered on the play's length; one critic, while acclaiming Shaw's achievement, observed nevertheless that "the play is verbose. It contains a good deal of fustian" (Evans, 278). Another reviewer,

Percy Hammond of the *Tribune*, found the work to be "just another example of Mr. Shaw's gift for interminable rag-chewing."[4] On the other hand, there were a number of favorable notices. The novelist Ludwig Lewisohn hailed the play as "obviously a first rate work by a first rate writer,"[5] and Heywood Broun announced that it was "the finest play written in the English language in our day."[6] The influential writer Alexander Woollcott told the readers of the *New York Herald* that the first-night audience "had seen a play that is beautiful, engrossing and at times [exalting]. They had seen certain scenes grow groggy for want of a blue pencil. . . . But it would be captious criticism and fraudulent reporting to give emphasis to such reservations when the outstanding thing is that a deathless legend came to life again on the Garrick's stage, quickened by the performance of a play that has greatness in it" (Evans, 275–76). The most excited reviewer was Jack Crawford, who declared that the theatrical season had given a play "which may not be equalled again in this age." "Plays the like of this one," he wrote, "occur at intervals of one hundred years apart, and once seen spoil the beholders for lesser stuff. This particular play is not only a triumph for the Theatre Guild, but also a milestone in the progress of the drama" (Tyson, 87).

The great Italian dramatist Luigi Pirandello was in the audience that opening night and wrote a commentary for the *New York Times*. He found that the play reflected Shaw's growing seriousness as an artist: "In none of Shaw's work that I can think of have considerations of art been so thoroughly respected as in *Saint Joan*." He goes on to discuss Shaw's conflict between poetry and polemic:

> There is a truly great poet in Shaw; but this combative Anglo-Irishman is often willing to forget that he is a poet, so immersed is he in being a citizen of his country, or a man of the twentieth century society, with a number of respectable ideas to defend, a number of sermons to preach, a number of antagonists to rout from the intellectual battlefield. But here, in *Saint Joan*, the poet comes into his own again, with only a subordinate role left, as a demanded compensation, to irony and satire. To be sure *Saint Joan* has all the savor and all the attractiveness of Shaw's witty polemical dialogue. But for all of these keen and cutting thrusts to left and right in Shaw's usual style of propaganda, *Saint Joan* is a work of poetry from beginning to end.

Pirandello ends with the observation that Shaw's fundamental positive puritanism—"which brooks no go-betweens and no mediations between man and God; a vigorous and independent vital energy, that frees itself restlessly and with joyous scorn from all the stupid and burdensome shackles of habit, routine and tradition, to conquer for itself a natural law more consonant with the poet's own being"—that this Puritanism is the same as Joan's, for she too cannot exist "without a life that is free and fruitful" (Evans, 281–84).[7]

Both the American and the British productions enjoyed extended runs, 213 performances in New York and 244 in London. One measure of the success of the play in pleasing Catholics as well as Protestants is that the American actress who played the lead, Winifred Lenihan, received a medal from New York's Cardinal Hayes. To someone who wondered whether Shaw might be turning Catholic, he quipped, "There's no room for two Popes in the Roman Catholic Church" (Pearson, 342).

The Paris production of the work was nearly ruined before it opened by a controversy in a Parisian drama magazine over whether the play insulted the French national heroine. Shaw joined in, testily scolding the French for their failure to appreciate his plays in the past:

> It seems to me that the theatre in France addresses itself less and less to an intelligent public; the public is in fact so stupid that an explanation of the play must be printed on the program to help the spectators to understand what they see. The other day I saw a program of *Arms and the Man* which carefully explains that the tragic figure of my play is a buffoon who must not be taken seriously. It is pitiful, because an appreciation of my plays in a way has become a proof of civilization. . . . If Paris perishes in ignorance of my work, the loss will be for Paris and not for me."[8]

Despite these efforts to ingratiate himself with the Parisian public, the modest Irishman had to endure a curious success when his play opened in Paris at the end of April, 1925. The celebrated actress Ludmilla Pitoeff scored a triumph in the leading role, but her interpretation ran counter to all that Shaw had intended. Joan's piety and fragility were emphasized; she became "a piteous little waif in her misery," and lacked those "insistent, energetic, almost pert, traits" (MacCarthy, 172), that Shaw had written into the script and had directed Sybil Thorndike to display. "What!" Shaw exclaimed to a friend who had praised Ludmilla's performance: "That frail, delicate woman is your idea of Joan of Arc? Joan of Arc was a strong peasant who could take a soldier by the scruff of the neck and throw him out the window. Your Mme Piroeff is charming, touching, but she would never have driven a single Englishman out of France" (Gerould, 210). Nonetheless, the Paris production ran for over 100 performances and was revived year after year for a decade. Its success perhaps proved that the dramatist had created a character multifaceted enough to sustain divergent portrayals.

Equally great triumphs awaited the play in Berlin, with Elisabeth Bergner featured in Max Reinhardt's production, and in Rome, Madrid, Belgrade, the Hague, Moscow (where they cut all words that suggested the miraculous nature of certain events), and as far afield as Tokyo. Since its opening, theaters throughout the world have continually revived *Saint Joan*, thus making it Shaw's most popular play.

It has also maintained its preeminence for the critics. Over the decades the play's high position in the Shaw canon has rarely been questioned. Commentators (such as Maurice Valency and W. H. Mason) have contented themselves with exploring the play's subtleties, while others (such as Margery Morgan and Louis Crompton) have elucidated the richness of its allusions. Reservations are occasionally expressed, as they were from the beginning, about the northern English dialect Shaw devised for Joan, about the belittling characterization he provided for the Dauphin, and especially about the appropriateness of the epilogue. But even when a dissenting critic, such as Kenneth Tynan, who finds grave faults in the script, actually sees a performance, he confesses himself moved to tears.[9] Joan remains one of the few great twentieth-century roles for young actresses.

Another interesting though marginal point of discussion for the critics is the play's genre. Shaw designated it as a chronicle play, and the theater historian Martin Meisel has further specified it as "a characteristic species of the nineteenth-century historical drama with which Shaw was entirely familiar: the heroic history play written for a woman star."[10] But the degree to which it is also a tragedy has been argued by a host of writers, most notably Sylvan

Barnett and Louis Martz. The matter is perhaps unresolvable since the work is in a distinctively mixed mode.

Unlike the relative unanimity over the work's theatrical power, debates over its historicity have occurred since its premiere, and Shaw himself in his 1924 preface to the play devoted several pages to defending its historical accuracy. But he failed to persuade English freethinker J. M. Robertson, who in 1926 devoted a small volume to exposing what he felt were Shaw's many historical errors.[11] A number of later commentators continue to take sides in the debate. The focus of the controversy is Shaw's characterization of the chief judge at Joan's trial, Bishop Cauchon: English critic A. M. Cohen, among more recent writers, finds Shaw elaborately inaccurate, whereas Brian Tyson, in a direct reply, finds Shaw's portrait of Cauchon completely valid. Seemingly this is an academic matter of interest only to specialists, but we shall see later on that the matter of fidelity to the records must influence our judgment of the meanings Shaw ascribed to his work.

Still, the indisputable impressiveness of Saint Joan as a play, its grand tribute by the resident of one country to the national hero of another, and its capping of a series of engaging plays extending back some 30 years, prompted the Nobel committee, finally, to give Shaw its award for literature for 1925. Quite apart from the play's happy fortunes in the world, we know that Joan continued to hold a special place in Shaw's heart; some years later, a sculptress neighbor of Shaw's, Clara Winston, made a statue of Joan that was placed in the garden of his country home, and it was beneath this statue that he directed that his cremated ashes be spread. It was a request fully observed when he died in 1950.

A READING

❖

In this section we must first attend to the dramaturgy—a dramaturgy that necessarily encompasses both the structure of the work and its dramatis personae. We then will pause over the vital issues embedded in the work, for Shaw took pride in being an intellectual dramatist who infused his plays with ideas, and Saint Joan is no exception. Next we will consider that curious appendage to the work known as the epilogue: longer than several of the preceding scenes, it has provoked much debate as to whether it enhances or detracts from the play proper. And after exploring this controversy, we will move on to scrutinize Shaw's claim in his preface that he was merely following the historical documents and dramatizing the true history of this famous woman, correcting thereby the misinterpretations of scores of other writers, including William Shakespeare, Friedrich von Schiller, Anatole France, and Mark Twain. This scrutiny of the play's historicity will, in turn, leave us with certain puzzles that can be solved only by considering Shaw himself and the ways in which his own temperamental needs and twentieth-century political dilemmas affected his portrait of Joan and her times. Finally, in a sort of epilogue, we will glance at an amusing and revealing episode in the play's subsequent career, as Shaw suddenly found himself, like his heroine, in conflict with high ecclesiastical authorities.

❖

4

The Structure

The pleasant shock of meeting Shaw's Joan is that she defies, with the help of the playwright, our stereotypical image of sainthood. Indeed, so successful is the dramatist in making her both magnetic and likable that we miss her when she is not around. A charming, earthy, robust, humorous, "unsaintly" saint seems paradoxical, but Shaw has certainly created one.

This Joan is at the center of the play that bears her name, and she radiates the entire circumference of the play. When not on stage, she is being talked about and reacted to. When present, she grips our attention. She has redeeming faults, often the obverse side of her virtues, and she suffers the penalties of success in a world of envious people whose self-importance she damages. She grows and changes before our eyes while yet remaining true to herself. We feel the play must come to an end when she dies because she has provided its life.

The creation of Joan is Shaw's greatest achievement in the work, and it stands quite apart from the question of whether the character's depiction is historically accurate. The play is theatrically compelling and is to be judged first and last as a work for the stage—as we also judge Shakespeare's "historical" plays. It is well to acknowledge this at the outset because so much that has been written about the play ignores the brilliance of its dramaturgy. Shaw himself in his role as essayist contributed to this waywardness, for his extended preface to the play deals with historical and philosophical matters of interest in themselves but largely irrelevant to the work we enjoy in the theater.

Designing the play's structure presented challenges to the dramatist equal to those of creating a plausible saint. Joan packed much activity into her brief public life and Shaw had to be very selective in choosing the incidents to dramatize. He boldly narrows the life down to six scenes and symmetrically gives three to Joan's rise and three to her fall. But the greatest structural problem he had was in her fall. Last acts in plays tend to be short: the curve of the action is terminating and matters are being wrapped up. This holds for Shaw's other plays and for Shakespeare's, as well. But Joan's life presented a peculiar pattern in that its greatest drama occurred in the trial at the end of her life, a trial that had its own beginning and middle and end. Shaw's task was to present, as it were, an entire short play at the end of the larger play, even introducing a handful of new characters to do so, and to manage this without unbalancing the first five scenes or marring the overall unity. It required severe selectivity and compression, and nothing better demonstrates Shaw's powers as a playwright than the way he carries this through. [1]

The three scenes devoted to Joan's fall bulk far larger in the play than those devoted to her rise, yet we actually see her for about the same length of time in each of the two sections. For nearly half the play she is offstage, and in only one of the scenes, the fifth, is she present from the beginning. This frequent absenting of the protagonist is one of the playwright's masterstrokes, for it both whets our appetite for her reappearance and suggests the passage of time. It also allows us to see her effects on others, as her deeds are discussed and strategies for controlling her are formulated. Given the wealth of events in her life, Shaw could easily have kept Joan on stage much longer, and his restraint from doing so obliged him to give her a telling presence when she does appear.

This art of omission—the phrase is Pascal's—prompted Shaw's boldest decision in selecting his incidents: the exclusion of Joan's military exploits. After all, it was her inspiriting of the French troops in battle and her prowess and courage in the field that gave credence to her claim that God was directing her. Shaw includes her boast to the French general that she, and not he, knows how to begin a battle and how to use the cannons; and Shaw allows her to grow nostalgic over the past excitement of capturing the bridge at Orléans. Yet he ignores the opportunity to show us any battle scenes. Why? Why, when every dramatist—Shakespeare is an instance—ordinarily loves such scenes because of their inherent action and conflict?

It was certainly not to avoid the expense of enlarging the cast that made Shaw omit the battle scenes, for such scenes do not require large numbers of men at all: any proficient playwright can convey the turmoil of fighting with just a few actors, and the cast of this play had enough supernumeraries to allow for a doubling of roles. (Shaw's own *Caesar and Cleopatra* includes fighting scenes.) Nor was it the lengthening of an already long play that dictated the omission, for such scenes require little talk and move swiftly. Nor was it the fact that Joan chose to carry the troop's standard rather than wield a weapon, for she deliberately carried the standard into the thick of the fighting. No, Shaw's decision was probably made for two reasons. First, he wanted his Joan to be distinct from Shakespeare's, who from her first appearance in *Henry VI, Part I* is portrayed as an Amazonian warrior hungry for battle. Even more important, he wanted to keep Joan before us as purely a victim of violence rather than surrounded by it. The excitement and climaxes of battle would have diminished the inner drama of her life, with its gathering despair, and diminished, too, the truly climactic trial scene. The play builds always toward that great last scene, and anything that would have robbed it of its excitement had to be excluded. One life alone is at stake in this play, and battle corpses would have lessened the pathos of that single death.

This is not to say, of course, that the preceding scenes do not have their own high points and drama. Every one of them does, to a lesser degree than the last scene, to be sure, but they are calculatingly there nonetheless. It is indeed one of the structural glories of the play that Shaw is able to give each of his scenes its own dramatic rhythms (and not only an expository, plot-advancing, or character-developing function), yet simultaneously to preserve the mounting momentum of the work as a whole.

Take the second scene as an example of the playwright's cunning in this regard. Essentially it repeats the pattern of the first scene on a larger scale: doubters of Joan's power test her and are then converted. Whereas the first scene's doubter was only one man, Captain Robert de Baudricourt, the later scene triples the number of skeptics and makes them men of greater social consequence: Gilles de Rais, Lord Chamberlain Trémouille, and (most intelligent of all) the Archbishop of Rheims. These men think they see through Joan and expect to make sport of her, yet by the end of the scene she has humbled de Rais and Trémouille and converted the Archbishop into a supporter. Three triumphs in a row, with yet a fourth to cap it—her instilling the Dauphin Charles with faith that he can become the consecrated king of France. Here is the climactic moment when Charles, with Joan at his side, finally asserts himself against the overbearing Trémouille, who has been the Dauphin's antagonist throughout the scene, cursing and insulting him, snatching a letter from his hand, and even raising a fist to him and making him hide behind the Archbishop:

> CHARLES [rising]. I have given the command of the army to The
> Maid. The Maid is to do as she likes with it. [He descends from
> the dais].
> General amazement. La Hire, delighted, slaps his steel thighpiece
> with his gauntlet.
> LA TRÉMOUILLE [turning threateningly towards Charles]. What is
> this? I command the army.
> Joan quickly puts her hand on Charles's shoulder as he instinc-
> tively recoils. Charles, with a grotesque effort culminating in an
> extravagant gesture, snaps his fingers in the Chamberlain's face.
> JOAN. Thou'rt answered, old Gruff-and-Grum. [Suddenly flashing
> out her sword as she divines that her moment has come.] Who is
> for God and His Maid? Who is for Orleans with me?
> LA HIRE [carried away, drawing also]. For God and His maid! To
> Orleans!
> ALL THE KNIGHTS [following his lead with enthusiasm]. To Orleans!
> Joan, radiant, falls on her knees in thanksgiving to God. They all
> kneel, except the Archbishop, who gives his benedictions with a
> sigh, and La Trémouille, who collapses, cursing. (2, 87)

Charles's boldness at this climactic moment is unexpected. We rejoice in the turning of the worm on his tormentor, and the comic struggle to snap his fingers intensifies our delight. Joan before our eyes has performed her greatest miracle yet: making a man out of Charles. The excitement of the soldier La Hire and of the knights confirms that a miracle has occurred, for the Archbishop has recently defined it as "an event which creates faith" (2, 78). Having seen this triumph of Joan's, we, too, can now believe in her powers and will not be surprised to hear of her later victories. Her cry "Who is for God," and her kneeling, show her devoutness. We ourselves almost want to follow her. Shaw has brilliantly aroused in us that heady mixture of idealism and bellicosity which makes us sense what the real Joan's powers must have been like.

Of course with part of our minds we resist this passage, with its melodramatic contrasts—the radiant heroine and the cursing villain, the suddenly converted knights—and we know it to be theatrical hokum. ("Flapdoodle" was Shaw's own word for it.[2]) But this is a play that somehow allows Shaw to use the dramatist's full palette, bright slashing colors here, quieter hues there. It is as if he is deliberately giving us medieval stained-glass effects, six colorful panels from the legendary life of a saint. Few works in the Shavian canon have such a range of effects, from the melodramatic to the disquisitional.

It is the latter that now appears in the next two scenes. Scene 3 comprises a conversation between Joan and the young general Dunois; scene 4—the tent scene—the conversation between the Earl of Warwick and the Bishop of Beauvais, with an occasional interruption from the English chaplain, John de Stogumber. These scenes are extraordinarily placed since the midsections of dramas are traditionally a high point of action, the peak of the mountain shape that playwrights favor. Shaw's diagrammatic model in this play seems more like a clothesline, weighted in the middle with talk. Nothing in Joan's career dictated this odd shape for the play; in fact, she does not appear in scene 4 at all, and it is the only one Shaw entirely invented. Nothing gives better proof of the playwright's discreet audacity than the apparently unconventional structure of the play, and this quite apart from the risk he took with the extended epilogue.

This seemingly odd shape has several advantages, however. The two middle conversational scenes contrast with the vigorous activity of the first two scenes and also with the two intense ones to come. Then again, variety is provided by the sheer reduction in the number of people on stage, the two scenes on either side of the middle ones being more populated, with the Dauphin Charles and his advisors in both of them. In a sense the two middle scenes form a sort of interlude and allow for a shift in mood.

There are, to be sure, significant differences between scenes 3 and 4. The brief third scene includes the sudden shift of the wind, the last of the miracles Shaw will include. The Maid's star is attaining its apogee. The fabulous events, the incredible romance of her swift rise to power and fame, are coming to an end. The real world, with its realpolitik, its vested interests, and its all-too-human creatures, emerges in the fourth scene and will, with mounting force, crush the innocent young woman. It is this rumble of menace beneath the cool political analyses of Warwick and Cauchon that makes this scene so different from the disquisitional passages in other Shavian plays such as *Candida* and *Getting Married*. Scene 4, in other words, for all its talk—or precisely because of the institutional power represented by the talkers—does subtly resemble the traditional mountain shape of a play after all, in that it marks the decisive turning point, and from here on Joan's star will hurtle downward.

Within this overarching action, each scene has its own well-wrought moments of suspense. In scene 1 we first wonder if Baudricourt will see the peasant girl and then if he will yield to her presumptuous command to be taken to the Dauphin. In scene 2, we have a triple barrage of suspense, first in whether Joan will be admitted to the court, then in whether she will recognize the Dauphin, and finally in whether he will give her troops to relieve the English siege of Orléans. In the quiet third scene, the pennon attached to Dunois's lance streams in a strong east wind, and the conversation both before and after Joan arrives centers on the need for the wind to change so that the boats can go upstream. But when Joan appears, we notice that the wind has stopped, because the pennon flaps down and hardly moves. Then, after a time, when Joan announces she will pray to Saint Catherine for a west wind, the pennon starts moving again—in the desired direction! (Shaw never used a stage prop more suspensefully.) In scene 4 we wonder whether the plans of Warwick and Cauchon against Joan will succeed, and in scene 5, whether Charles will back her proposal to attack Paris or everyone will now abandon her. Finally, in the powerful last scene, Shaw rouses our uncertainty many times: will Joan be tortured? will she yield to the clerics and renounce her voices? will she suffer any penalty after her recantation? will she withdraw her recantation? will she really be burnt alive?

Connoisseurs of dramaturgy will notice, too, the adroitness with which Shaw prolongs the suspense here and there. A fine instance occurs in the last scene just after Joan recants:

> JOAN [*despairing*]. Oh, it is true: it is true; my voices have deceived me. I have been mocked by devils: my faith is broken. I have dared and dared: but only a fool will walk into a fire: God, who gave me commonsense, cannot will me to do that. .
>
> LADVENU. Now God be praised that He has saved you at the eleventh hour! [*He hurries to the vacant seat at the scribes' table, and snatches a sheet of paper, on which he sets to work writing eagerly.*] (6, 142)

Ladvenu could have had the recantation paper ready—in the actual event it *was* ready—but Shaw wants to extend this moment. Perhaps Joan will change her mind? We watch her sitting there, gloomy and diminished. And how at this somber juncture does the playwright fill the time while Ladvenu is writing? With a daring bit of farce comedy! The obtuse Chaplain Stogumber rises in furious protest at Joan's escaping the stake. He accuses the assembled churchmen of betraying the Cardinal of Winchester and the Earl of Warwick. He shouts that the English soldiers outside will burn Joan no matter what she does. The assessors voice astonishment at this outburst and then the Inquisitor speaks:

> THE INQUISITOR [*rising*]. Silence, pray! Gentlemen: pray silence! Mater Chaplain: bethink you a moment of your holy office: of what you are, and where you are. I direct you to sit down.
>
> THE CHAPLAIN [*folding his arms doggedly, his face working convulsively*]. I will NOT sit down.
>
> CAUCHON. Master Inquisitor: this man has called me a traitor to my face before now.
>
> THE CHAPLAIN. So you are a traitor. You are all traitors. You have been doing nothing but begging this damnable witch on your knees to recant all through this trial.
>
> THE INQUISITOR [*placidly resuming his seat*]. If you will not sit, you must stand: that is all.
>
> THE CHAPLAIN. I will NOT stand [*he flings himself back into his chair*].
>
> LADVENU [*rising with the paper in his hand*]. My lord: here is the form of recantation for The Maid to sign. (6, 143)

And Ladvenu proceeds to read the solemn recantation quietly—the solemnity and quietness heightened by Stogumber's previous shouting.

Now, the manipulation of suspense is counterpointed by its resolution; modern dramatists, whose acts usually terminate with the dropping of a curtain, like to build toward a vivid final moment—a strong "curtain." This may involve simply a resolution of suspense, or its heightening, or, most intricately, a resolution that also creates new suspense. In five of the six scenes in our play, we can notice that Shaw has very strong curtains indeed. "Miracles" climax the first three scenes—Charles's transformation being an even more improbable miracle than the egg laying—and each of these curtains is of the intricate type that stimulates future uncertainties even as it resolves present suspense. So, too, is the end of scene 4, where after a good deal of guarded talk, the representatives of the church and the baronage come to a decisive agreement; and of course the last scene climaxes with Joan's burning. Only in scene 5 do we have a limp curtain, and this is marvelously appropriate, for Joan and the King are now at odds, and the downbeat ending reflects the ragged morale of the court.

Joan's burning is not the only climax of the final curtain. Amid the final fireworks, Shaw explodes three stunning surprises: after Joan has been hurried off to the stake, the Inquisitor announces that she is quite innocent; then Stogumber, the intemperate jingoist, unexpectedly staggers back with sobs of remorse issuing from his lips, aghast at having seen a fellow creature burned alive; and then Warwick, when the executioner reports that Joan is dead and the last has now been heard of her, says with a wry smile, in the play's final line, "The last of her? Hm! I wonder!"

The structure of the play is further enhanced throughout by Shaw's skillful use of *foreshadowing*. In the very first scene, for example, Robert de Baudricourt replies to his steward's announcement that Joan has put a spell on them, that they are bewitched, with the remark that he burns witches. The Dauphin warns Joan in the next scene that although she has put courage into him and he will take risks, "I shant be able to keep it up" (2, 86), a warning that prepares us to accept his relapse to timidity later in the play when he turns against her. In the same scene, there is some discussion of the failure to raise the English siege of Orléans, and La Hire says that the wind is blowing the wrong way to ship the troops up the Loire: "[Dunois] is tired of paying the priests to pray for a west wind. What he needs is a miracle" (2, 77). The miracle is achieved in the next scene as Joan talks to Dunois, and the priests' failure to do what Joan does indicates another reason for their later resentment of her.

Again, Dunois, before Joan arrives, is bird-watching with his page and spots a blue kingfisher in the reeds. When the page says he wishes he could catch the kingfishers, Dunois scolds him: "Let me catch you trying to trap them, and I will put you in the iron cage for a month to teach you what a cage feels like" (3, 89). This, of course, not only reveals something of Dunois's character, but also subtly prepares us for the end of the play, with Joan justifying her attempt to flee from prison with the remark, "If you leave the door of the cage open the bird will fly out" (6, 134), and with her preference of death to life imprisonment because being caged in prison "would shut me from the light of the sky and the sight of the fields and flowers" (6, 145). The end of the fifth scene is heavy with warnings of Joan's impending fate as the Archbishop and Dunois and the King take turns telling her how hopeless her condition will be if she is captured.

These and other foreshadowings are matched in the latter part of the work by reminiscences that heighten the pathos of her current state, as when she sighs to Dunois her wish that they were fighting at the bridge at Orléans again: "we *lived* at that bridge" (5, 109). Later, she recalls attacking the English at Orléans: "You locked the gates to keep me in; and it was the townsfolk and the common people that followed me, and forced the gate, and shewed the way to fight in earnest" (5, 116). It is through such anticipations and recollections that Shaw helps bind the parts of the play together.

Recurrent allusions also work cohesively. Joan asks Charles in the second scene, "Wilt be a poor little Judas, and betray me and Him that sent me?" and, a moment later, "Art for or against me?" (2, 286). Through these lines Shaw hints at parallels between Joan and Jesus; such parallels become more frequent toward the end, and especially in the epilogue. (Margery Morgan calls attention to the intimation of the harrowing of hell in the soldier's day off from hell for his kindness to Joan; to Stogumber's resemblance to doubting Thomas in his need to see with his own eyes before he can believe; to the biblical echo in Joan's line "Woe unto me when all men praise me!"—the original in Luke 6:26 reading "Woe unto you, when all men shall speak well of you! for so did their fathers to the false prophets."[3]) Given these specific parallels between Jesus and Joan—a conjunction of names that Shaw also made when lecturing on the play[4]—we might go further and contemplate some other ones, such as their both being ahead of their times in doctrine, their sense of mission, their service to a higher power, their willingness to die for their cause, the miracles that attend them, their loneliness, their effect on other people, their earthly fate and later fame. The differences, such as Joan's militancy, should also be noted, though as we saw earlier, Shaw does keep the military activities well offstage. The playwright is not at all indicating a one-to-one equivalence between Jesus and Joan—to do so would be mutually inappropriate—but is merely suggesting a Christian context. He enriches that context by occasionally placing Joan into referential juxtaposition with the Virgin Mary in the second and third scenes.

A special structural challenge presented by Joan's story lay in her miracles, her visions and her voices. Shaw knew that many people in a modern audience would find these hard to accept, and he himself accepted them only in a special, non-Catholic sense, which he elucidated in the preface. To omit them from the play, however, would have been to falsify her story, just as to discredit them would have discredited her. Shaw met this challenge in varied and ingenious ways.

He first makes us believe in the most impressive miracle of all, Joan herself. "I think the girl herself is a bit of a miracle," Poulengey announces in scene 1, and the first half of the play shows people whose skepticism toward her is overcome by her powers. These include two types of "miracles," the greater being the restoration of men's faith in themselves: she inspirits them from the overflow of her belief in the cause. The lesser miracles, such as the hens' sudden burst of egg laying or the sudden shift in the wind, are merely external and possibly coincidental. In fact, if a miracle is considered an infringement of ordinary natural laws, then hens who refuse to lay and an east wind that blows for days are more extraordinary than is the return of the natural order that accompanies Joan's presence. (Notice that the wind shifts *before* Joan can fulfill Dunois's request to pray for it.) These events hover between the natural and the supernatural, and they can be taken in one way by skeptics and another by believers. Shaw deals with them with humane discretion—though both times he is shameless dramatist enough to exploit them for strong curtains.

Shaw soothes the skeptics in his audience, and perhaps his own non-Christian conscience, by allowing for the possibility that miracles are only apparent. He puts into the mouth of the worldly Archbishop of Rheims the view that most miracles can have a quite naturalistic explanation; but as long as this is not known to the believer, it does not matter. "If they confirm or create faith they are true miracles," says the churchman. "When this girl picks out the Dauphin among his courtiers, it will not be a miracle for me, because I shall know how it has been done, and my faith will not be increased. But as for the others, if they feel the thrill of the supernatural, and forget their sinful clay in a sudden sense of the glory of God, it will be a miracle and a blessed one" (2, 79).

Shaw similarly does his highwire balancing act with Joan's visions and voices. Since her sincerity is undisputable, we believe that she does see Saint Margaret and Saint Catherine and hear their voices, but whether these "are real persons or illusions," as Shaw wrote to a friend, was left "an open question to retain the interest of the modernists" in the audience (*CL*, 3:897). Yet he dares to give us one moment when Joan actually hears a voice. It is wisely a moment well into the play, when we already utterly believe in her integrity, and she does not boast but rather confides to her friend Dunois what is happening. She is alone with him in the ambulatory of the cathedral of Rheims and becomes rapt as the clock strikes the quarter hour. She hears a voice within the sound saying, "Dear child of God," and wonders whether Dunois hears it too. (Subtly, Shaw hints that the words may be an echo produced on her sensitive imagination, for Dunois has called her a child of God a few moments earlier, as she herself reminds him.) As she continues to speak excitedly of her voices, the young general interrupts her: "You make me uneasy when you talk about your voices: I should think you were a bit cracked if I hadn't noticed that you give me very sensible reasons for what you do" (5, 111). This notion of inspired good sense is repeated by Joan, perhaps again because of her impressionability, when she retorts a little later to the Archbishop: "When have they [my voices] ever lied: If you will not believe in them: even if they are only the echoes of my own commonsense, are they not always right? and are not your earthly counsels always wrong?" (5, 118). Shaw has Joan go even one step further in accepting the skeptic's view of her voices when she replies to Baudricout's accusation that her voices do not come from God but only from her imagination: "Of course. That is how the messages of God come to us" (1, 67). Whether the real Joan would have made such a statement is extremely doubtful, but Shaw allows his stage Joan to go far toward accommodating a secular view of her supernatural revelations without for a moment herself denying their reality.

5

The Men

The 20 males in the play cover a broad social spectrum, from servants to kings. The soldiers range from the slow-speaking, lymphatic Bertrand de Poulengey, through the energetic but weak-willed Baudricourt, to the dapper, self-possessed de Rais (Bluebeard) and the good-natured, capable Dunois. (These descriptive terms are largely Shaw's own, and indicate the care he took to create a variety of contrasting types.) The churchmen range from the routine-minded petty Canon Courcelles, through the prosecutor D'Estivet—"well-mannered, but vulpine beneath his veneer"—to the humane, "ascetically fine-drawn Dominican," Ladvenu. The Inquisitor, Lemaître, is a mild, elderly gentlemen with reserves of authority and firmness, the very opposite of the excitable, bigoted Stogumber. The two high ecclesiastics, the Archbishop of Rheims and the Bishop of Beauvais (Monseigneur Cauchon), are also contrasted, the former a political prelate and the latter a pious man devoted to the well-being of the Church. Shaw has time and opportunity, with a cast of this size, for only limited characterization, and only a handful of the males receive any rounded treatment. Despite this, Shaw breathes life and individuality even into such minor figures as the steward in the first scene and the page in the third, and he allows a moment of vividness to the one woman in the play other than Joan who has a speaking part—the Duchess de la Trémouille—though it is only a few words. Joan is kneeling in the Duchess's way:

> THE DUCHESS [coldly]. Will you allow me to pass, please?
> JOAN. Be that Queen?

CHARLES. No. She thinks she is.

JOAN [*Again staring after the Duchess*]. Oo-oo-ooh! [*Her awestruck amazement at the figure cut by the magnificently dressed lady is not wholly complimentary*].

LA TRÉMOUILLE [*very surly*]. I'll trouble your highness not to gibe at my wife. (2, 83)

This is a small passage, admittedly, but one that establishes a contrast with the country girl simple in dress and manner. It also shows Joan's assertiveness even with the high and mighty, since the Duchess earlier had sneered at Joan's hairstyle.

Many of the men, or rather their imperfections, are used to highlight Joan's virtues. Thus, her willpower when we first meet her is made more impressive by the blustering irresoluteness of Captain de Baudricourt, her purposefulness and selflessness are emphasized by the contrasting timorousness and hedonism of the Dauphin, and her piety shines forth against the worldliness of the Archbishop.

This Archbishop is one of the half dozen men who are characterized in some depth. At first we see him as an extremely worldly prelate, a man who uses his imposing bearing and authority of office to bully the King. He is shrewd and somewhat cynical, confiding to the Lord Chamberlain that most miracles are simply "innocent contrivances by which the priest fortifies the faith of his flock" (2, 79). For a miracle need not actually emanate from a divine source as long as people think it does and as long as it confirms or creates faith—a position that the Lord Chamberlain rightly says "seems a bit fishy to me" (2, 78). Nevertheless, this rationalistic prelate, who would rather be reading Aristotle and Pythagoras than attending to saints and their miracles, is deeply moved when Joan kneels to him and asks his blessing, and a moment afterwards surprisingly says he is unworthy of the honor.

Less worldly is the Bishop of Beauvais, Peter Cauchon, the most elaborately developed prelate in the play. An honorable and devout man, with a quick temper, he is dedicated wholly to the authority of the Church and passionately defends its role in preserving civilization:

What will the world be like [he asks Warwick] when The Church's accumulated wisdom and knowledge and experience, its councils of learned, venerable pious men, are thrust into the kennel by every ignorant laborer or dairymaid whom the devil can puff up with the monstrous self-conceit of being directly inspired from heaven? It will be a world of blood, of fury, of devastation, of each man striving for his own hand: in the end a world wrecked back into barbarism. For now you have only Mahomet and his dupes, and the Maid and her dupes; but what will it be when every girl thinks herself a Joan and every man a Mahomet? I shudder to the very marrow of my bones when I think of it." (4, 103)

At first, Warwick mistakenly thinks that Bishop Cauchon is as eager as he is to burn Joan as a witch. He is actually startled at the Bishop's concern for Joan's soul: "No, my lord: the soul of this village girl is of equal value with yours or your king's before the throne of God; and my first duty is to save it. . . . I am no mere political bishop: my faith is to me what your honor is to you; and if there be a loophole through which this baptized child of God can creep to her salvation, I shall guide her to it" (4, 101).

Cauchon manifests this solicitude for Joan's spiritual well-being in the courtroom scene. He fiercely rebukes Warwick's threat to kill Joan as a political necessity whatever the outcome of the trial, insisting that "the Church is not subject to political necessity" (6, 125). He rebukes Canon Courcelles for wanting to put Joan to the customary tortures and strives to lead Joan gently to repentance:

> CAUCHON. Joan, I am going to put a most solemn question to you.
> Take care how you answer; for your life and salvation are at
> stake on it. Will you for all you have said and done, be it good
> or bad, accept the judgment of God's Church on earth? More
> especially as to the acts and words that are imputed to you in
> this trial by the Promoter here, will you submit your case to the
> inspired interpretation of the Church Militant?'
> JOAN. I am a faithful child of The Church. I will obey The
> Church—
> CAUCHON [hopefully leaning forward]. You will?
> JOAN. —provided it does not command anything impossible.
> *Cauchon sinks back in his chair with a heavy sigh.* (6, 136)

When Joan does recant, Cauchon echoes Ladvenu's thanks to God for saving her. When Joan withdraws her recantation and is rushed out to the stake, he protests the indecent haste and scolds Warwick for not observing the proper forms; later, he resists going out to see the "dreadful thing" that they are doing to the girl. Throughout, he is shown to be a merciful and high-minded prelate, whose purity of motives in seeking to help Joan while protecting the Church's authority equals her own selfless idealism. Shaw has created an entirely worthy, and blameless, antagonist for Joan, though, as we shall see later, he may be an idealized version of the real Bishop Cauchon.

Less high-minded, though comparably astute and more religiously tolerant, is the Earl of Warwick, the suave and imposing representative of the English forces in France. A well-traveled soldier apologetic that his battle-hardened sensibilities make him seem callous to the prospective burning of a young woman, Warwick defends the prerogatives of his class, the feudal lords, against the principle he believes Joan upholds, the divine right of kings. In the superb matching of wits of the fourth scene, Warwick shows himself Cauchon's equal in eloquence and his better in self-control. In type he harks back to General "Gentleman Johnny" Burgoyne of *The Devil's Disciple*, though he is more rugged and determined.

Joan's only friend among the primary men in the play is the young general Dunois, known as the Bastard of Orléans because he is the natural son of Louis, Duke of Orléans. He is at first patient and gentle with Joan, amused by her indifference to his rank and responding in kind to her tone of familiarity. He instructs her in military matters and is in turn overwhelmed by her apparent power to change the wind's direction. He kneels to her and hands her his general's baton, saying, "You command the king's army. I am your soldier" (3, 93). Together they win the critical fight at Orléans and then the lesser battles on the road to Charles's coronation at Rheims. There, however, we see an interesting development in Dunois's relationship with Joan. Though they have been comrades in arms, she has been given all the credit for the victories. His hard work in finding troops and feeding them has gone unregarded. He knows, as he says to the king, "exactly how much God did for us through The Maid, and how much He left me to do by my own wits" (5, 115). Joan is not sensitive to this understandable touch of jealousy, and she publicly insults his military abilities: "You don't know how to begin a battle; and you don't know how to use your cannons" (5, 115). She herself knows both these things, she brags. Dunois counters by reminding her that their victories have been helped by having superior numbers; and he warns her presciently that if she attacks Compiègne with insufficient forces she may be captured because "God is on the side of the big battalions" (5, 117). Dunois's criticisms of the young woman carry more weight with us than those of anyone else in the play, since he admires her and has befriended her. We believe him when he speaks his ominous final words, "As God is my judge, if she fell into the Loire I would jump in in full armor to fish her out. But if she plays the fool at Compiègne, and gets caught, I must leave her to her doom" (5, 120). It was, we recall, in the assault at Compiègne, with insufficient troops, that Joan was finally captured.

The King does not attempt to ransom her. But we sense from the personality that Shaw has sketched for us why Charles deserts her. He is a weak man, but with an engaging frankness about his limitations. Shaw uses him to the point of caricature for delicious comedy. Though Charles has neither Falstaff's bulk nor his wit, he shares with Shakespeare's great Sir John an outlook determinedly antiheroic. All these big soldiers, he complains, "like fighting: most of them are making fools of themselves all the time they are not fighting; but I am quiet and sensible; and I don't want to kill people: I only want to be left alone to enjoy myself in my own way. I never asked to be a king: it was pushed on me" (2, 138). When Joan, in love with all the virtues, assures Charles that she will put courage into him, he replies sharply: "But I don't want to have courage put into me. I want to sleep in a comfortable bed, and not live in continual terror of being killed or wounded. Put courage into the others, and let them have their bellyful of fighting; but let me alone" (2, 84). He honestly admits that he is ugly, that he hates his son—"a horrid boy"—and is fed up with religion: "Oh do stop talking about God and praying. I can't bear people who are always praying. Isn't it bad enough to have to do it at the proper times?" (2, 85). When Joan offers him a message direct from God, he shakes his head and retorts, "I don't want a message" (2, 85). But he will allow her to tip him off to any cures she knows. Or if she can do the alchemist's trick of turning lead into gold, he will be delighted to learn it. When, despite himself, he is officially thrust into the kingship and is crowned at Rheims, he moans about the combined weight of the coronation robes and the crown, and protests that the famous holy oil was rancid—he still cannot get its stink out of his nostrils. Amazed at the victories his troops have had, he is eager to stop fighting before his luck turns, and to make a quick treaty and ship Joan back to her village as soon as possible. Charles provides the play with much royal amusement.

A final source of character comedy is the English Chaplain, John de Stogumber. He is cunningly used by Shaw for expository purposes but of course it is his personality that most amuses us. He bears a certain resemblance, as several commentators have noted, to Britannicus, the secretary in *Caesar and Cleopatra*, yet the resemblance is superficial, consisting mainly in a shared pride in being English. Britannicus is stiff, controlled, obsessed with propriety, whereas Stogumber is moody, contentious and excitable, a man who bursts beyond social forms, screams to Bishop Cauchon that he is a traitor, screams later to the assessors that they are all traitors. His simple mind cannot keep pace with his vehemence, and he is always stumbling into misunderstandings. As a bull-necked, truculent priest, he is a study of a man professionally miscast, a cousin of that Ferrovius in *Androcles and the Lion* who cannot school his temper to Christian meekness. Stogumber is also an uninhibited chauvinist, convinced that the English were defeated in battle only because Joan is a sorceress, and insisting "We were not fairly beaten, my lord. No Englishman is ever fairly beaten" (4, 97). When Cauchon contemptuously remarks that all Englishmen are "born heretics," Stogumber responds with confused outrage: "How can what an Englishman believes be heresy? It is a contradiction in terms" (4, 104). He is astonished that Joan does not accept England's right to conquer—a right, he declares, given the country by God "because of her peculiar fitness to rule over less civilized races for their own good" (4, 108). He knows that Joan is lying about her voices because she says that the blessed saints Margaret and Catherine and the Archangel Michael spoke to her in French, and naturally they would speak in the superior tongue—English.

Stogumber also appears to be a sadistic man, growling in the fourth scene that he would like to burn Joan with his own hands and fearful in the last scene that she will escape the stake. "Into the fire with the witch," he shouts gleefully as he helps the soldiers remove her from the court. But Stogumber's sadism, Shaw deftly reveals, is mixed with other elements, his cruel words equally prompted by hotheadedness and a torpid imagination. In one of the play's most inspired passages, Stogumber staggers back into the courtroom just after Joan's martyrdom, sobbing with remorse and guilt. "I meant no harm," he moans. "I did not know what it would be like." And he laments in a tearful voice:

> I let them do it. If I had known, I would have torn her from their hands. You don't know: you haven't seen: it is so easy to talk when you don't know. You madden yourself with words: you damn yourself because it feels grand to throw oil on the flaming hell of your own temper. But when it is brought home to you: when you see the thing you have done; when it is blinding your eyes, stifling your nostrils, tearing your heart, then—then— [*Falling to his knees*] O God, take away this sight from me! O Christ, deliver me from this fire that is consuming me! She cried to Thee in the midst of it: Jesus! Jesus! Jesus! She is in Thy bosom; and I am in hell evermore. (6, 149)

And then, right after these agitated lines, Shaw wonderfully lets the distraught chaplain find some solace in his nationality, as he recounts that as Joan moved towards the stake a merciful soldier gave her two sticks tied together in a makeshift cross: "Thank God he was an Englishman! I might have done it: but I did not: I am a coward, a mad dog, a fool. But he was an Englishman too" (6, 149). And we smile as he then declares, with the surviving other side of his chauvinism, that the people who laughed at her must have been French.

Many critics have dismissed Stogumber as a wretched caricature, but Pirandello is quite right in insisting that he is one of the work's greatest creations. As the Italian writer put it after seeing the world premiere in New York: "Much more free and unobstructed in his natural impulses [than Joan], much more independent of any deliberate restraints, and accordingly much more 'living' (from my point of view) is the Chaplain, de Stogumber, the truly admirable creation in this drama, and a personage on which Shaw has surely expended a great deal of affectionate effort." Any other dramatist, he believes, would have lowered the curtain at the moment Joan is taken out to the stake:

> But Shaw cannot resist the pressure and the inspiration of the life he well knows must be surging in such circumstances in his

other character—the Chaplain. He rushes on towards a second
climax of not less noble poetry, depicting with magnificent elan
the mad remorse, the hopeless penitence of Stogumber, thus
adding to our first crisis of exquisite anguish another not less
potent and overwhelming" (Evans, 283).

In the tent scene, this blunt emotional man serves as a vital foil to
the calculating Earl of Warwick, and he provides comic relief to the
political and theological analyses of Warwick and Cauchon; in the
final scene he brings in necessary news of Joan's last minutes even
as he rises to his own epiphany. His weaknesses strengthen the
play.

6

The Maid

Against the backdrop of the play's various mature men, Joan's innocence and youthfulness stand out conspicuously. She is of
course the most superlatively imagined figure in the work, sharply
defined yet multifaceted. Her ingenuousness and occasional naivete
are balanced by her quick-wittedness and great common sense.
Shaw's first description of her—as an able-bodied country girl with
a resolute mouth and a fighting chin, and a hearty, coaxing
voice—emphasizes her earthiness rather than her piety, but it is
made clear that her confidence derives from her sense of servitude
to God. Recall her words when she first appears, summoned to the
stone chamber of Baudricourt's castle:

> JOAN [*bobbing a curtsey*]. Good morning, captain squire. Captain:
>   you are to give me a horse and armor and some soldiers, and
>   send me to the Dauphin. Those are your orders from my Lord.
> ROBERT [*outraged*]. Orders from *your* lord! And who the devil may
>   your lord be? Go back to him, and tell him that I am neither
>   duke nor peer at his orders: I am squire Baudricourt; and I
>   take no orders except from the king.
> JOAN [*reassuringly*]. Yes, squire: that is all right. My Lord is the
>   King of Heaven.
> ROBERT. Why, the girl's mad. [*To the steward*] Why didn't you tell
>   me so, you blockhead?
> STEWARD. Sir: do not anger her: give her what she wants.
> JOAN [*impatient but friendly*]. They all say I am mad until I talk to
>   them, squire. But you see that it is the will of God that you are
>   to do what He has put into my mind.

ROBERT. It is the will of God that I shall send you back to your father with orders to put you under lock and key and thrash the madness out of you. What have you to say to that?

JOAN. You think you will, squire; but you will find it all coming quite different. You said you would not see me; but here I am. . . .

ROBERT. Now listen to me, I am going to assert myself.

JOAN [*busily*]. Please do, squire. The horse will cost sixteen francs. It is a good deal of money; but I can save it on the armor. I can find a soldier's armor that will fit me well enough: I am very hardy; and I do not need beautiful armor made to my measure like you wear. I shall not want many soldiers: the Dauphin will give me all I need to raise the siege of Orleans.

ROBERT [*flabbergasted*]. To raise the siege of Orleans!

JOAN [*simply*]. Yes, squire: that is what God is sending me to do.
    (1, 60–61)

The outrageousness of Joan's claims and intentions would be intolerable were it not for the force of her personality, "her magnetic field," as Shaw termed it in a stage direction. And this combination of innocence and confidence in her heaven-sent mission fascinates the spectator as much as it does Robert, whose skepticism reflects our own. She could easily be dismissed as a wandering village idiot were it not for her knack of restoring men's faith in themselves and the odd way nature behaves when she passes by: the hens resume their egg laying after an unwonted layoff, and the west wind breezes back into action after a lengthy absence.

Shaw invented this conversation with Baudricourt, but he captured the flavor of Joan's style from verbatim transcripts of her actual trial, which he studied while preparing the play. He stated quite correctly that many of the lines in the play were taken with little change from these documents. It may be of interest to look for a moment at a few of the pages that Shaw read and to see how he transformed them for theatrical purposes. For example, at the trial Joan was asked why she had tried to escape from one of the prisons in which she had been held, and she answered:

"Never was I prisoner in such a place that I would not willingly have escaped. Being in that Castle, I should have shut my keepers in the tower, if it had not been that the porter espied me and encountered me. It did not please God that I should escape this time: it was necessary for me to see the English King, as my Voices had told me, as has been already said."

"Have you had permission from God or your Voices to leave prison when it shall please you?"

"I have asked it many times, but I have not yet had it."

"Would you go now, if you saw your starting-point?"

"If I saw the door open, I should go: that would be leave from Our Lord. If I saw the door open, and my keepers and the other English beyond power of resistance, truly I should see in it my leave and help sent me by Our Lord. But without this leave, I shall not go, unless I make a forcible attempt to go, and so learn if Our Lord would be pleased: this on the strength of the proverb, 'Help thyself, and God will help thee': I say this in order that, if I do escape, no one may say I did so without God's leave."[1]

Shaw catches some of the wit and common sense, if not the piety, of Joan's reply in the following passage, which also gives a sense of his skill in compression:

> D'ESTIVET. Why did you leave the tower?
> JOAN. Why would anybody leave a prison if they could get out?
> D'ESTIVET. You tried to escape?
> JOAN. Of course I did; and not for the first time either. If you leave the door of the cage open the bird will fly out.
> D'ESTIVET [rising]. That is a confession of heresy. I call the attention of the court to it.
> JOAN. Heresy, he calls it! Am I a heretic because I try to escape from prison?
> D'ESTIVET. Assuredly, if you are in the hands of The Church, and you willfully take yourself out of its hands, you are deserting The Church: and that is heresy.
> JOAN. It is great nonsense. Nobody could be such a fool as to think that. (6, 133–34)

For another instance, let us take the account in the documents of Joan's premonition that she would be captured:

"During the Easter week of last year, being in the trenches of Melun, it was told me by my Voices—that is to say, by Saint Catherine and Saint Margaret—'Thou wilt be taken before Saint John's Day; and so it must be: do not torment thyself about it; be resigned; God will help thee.' "

"Before this occasion at Melun, had not your Voices ever told you that you would be taken?"

"Yes, many times and nearly every day. And I asked of my Voices that, when I should be taken, I might die soon, without long suffering in prison; and they said to me: 'Be resigned to all—this it must be.' But they did not tell me the time; and if I had known it, I should not have gone. Often I asked to know the hour: they never told me." (Murray, 57–58)

In the play, Shaw is forced to reduced this sweet and naive response to a minimum but nevertheless conveys Joan's wistfulness:

JOAN. La Hire: in spite of all your sins and swears we shall meet in heaven; for I love you as I love Pitou, my old sheep dog. Pitou could kill a wolf. You will kill the English wolves until they go back to their country and become good dogs of God, will you not?

LA HIRE. You and I together: yes.

JOAN. No: I shall last only a year from the beginning.

ALL THE OTHERS. What!

JOAN. I know it somehow. (5, 112)

Shaw occasionally emphasizes for dramatic purposes some of Joan's straightforward replies. When she was asked whether she was in the grace of God, Joan replied, "If I am not, may God place me there; if I am, may God so keep me. I should be the saddest in all the world if I knew that I were not in the grace of God. But if I were in a state of sin, do you think the Voice would come to me?" (Murray, 18). In the play Shaw cuts and expands this as follows:

CAUCHON. Dare you pretend, after what you have said, that you are in a state of grace?

JOAN. If I am not, may God bring me to it: if I am, may God keep me in it!

LADVENU. That is a very good reply, my lord.

COURCELLES. Were you in a state of grace when you stole the Bishop's horse? (6, 138)

As a final example of how Shaw stays close to the records but heightens their dramatic power, let us look at the climactic moment in the documents when Joan is asked whether she will obey the Church:

> "Will you refer yourself to the judgment of the Church on earth for all you have said or done, be it good or bad? Especially will you refer to the Church the cases, crimes, and offences which are imputed to you and everything which touches on this Trial?"
>
> "On all that I am asked I will refer to the Church Militant, provided they do not command anything impossible. And I hold as a thing impossible to declare that my actions and my words and all that I have answered on the subject of my visions and revelations I have not done and said by the order of God; this, I will not declare for anything in the world. And that which God hath made me do, hath commanded or shall command, I will not fail to do for any man alive. It would be impossible for me to revoke it. And in case the Church should wish me to do anything contrary to the command which has been given me of God, I will not consent to it, whatever it may be."
>
> "If the Church Militant tells you that your revelations are illusions, or diabolical things, will you defer to the Church?"
>
> "I will defer to God, Whose Commandments I always do. I know well that that which is contained in my Case has come to me by the Commandment of God; what I affirm in the Case is, that I have acted by the order of God; it is impossible for me to say otherwise. In case the Church should prescribe the contrary, I should not refer to any one in the world, but to God alone, Whose Commandment I always follow."
>
> "Do you not then believe you are subject to the Church of God which is on earth, that is to say to our Lord the Pope, to the Cardinals, the Archbishops, Bishops, and other prelates of the Church?"
>
> "Yes, I believe myself to be subject to them; but God must be served first."
>
> "Have you then command from your Voices not to submit yourself to the Church Militant, which is on earth, nor to its decision?"
>
> "I answer nothing from my own head; what I answer is by command of my Voices; they do not order me to disobey the Church, but God must be served first." (Murray, 103–4)

Shaw's version follows this closely except for the very end:

> CAUCHON. Come! We are wasting time on trifles. Joan: I am going to put a most solemn question to you. Take care how you an-

swer; for your life and salvation are at stake on it. Will you for all you have said and done, be it good or bad, accept the judgment of God's Church on earth? More especially as to the acts and words that are imputed to you in this trial by the Promoter here, will you submit your case to the inspired interpretation of the Church Militant?

JOAN. I am a faithful child of The Church. I will obey The Church—

CAUCHON [*Hopefully leaning forward*]. You will?

JOAN. —provided it does not command anything impossible.

Cauchon sinks back in his chair with a heavy sigh. The Inquisitor purses his lips and frowns. Ladvenu shakes his head pitifully.

D'ESTIVET. She imputes to The Church the error and folly of commanding the impossible.

JOAN. If you command me to declare that all that I have done and said, and all the visions and revelations I have had, were not from God, then that is impossible: I will not declare it for anything in the world. What God made me do I will never go back on; and what He has commanded or shall command I will not fail to do in spite of any man alive. That is what I mean by impossible. And in case The Church should bid me do anything contrary to the command I have from God, I will not consent to it, no matter what it may be.

THE ASSESSORS [*shocked and indignant*]. Oh! The Church contrary to God! What do you say now? Flat heresy. This is beyond everything, etc, etc.

D'ESTIVET [*throwing down his brief*]. My lord: do you need anything more than this?

CAUCHON. Woman: you have said enough to burn ten heretics. Will you not be warned? Will you not understand?

THE INQUISITOR. If the Church Militant tells you that your revelations and visions are sent by the devil to tempt you to your damnation, will you not believe that The Church is wiser than you?

JOAN. I believe that God is wiser than I; and it is His commands that I will do. All the things that you call my crimes have come to me by the command of God. I say that I have done them by the order of God; it is impossible for me to say anything else. If any Churchman says the contrary I shall not mind him: I shall mind God alone, whose command I always follow.

LADVENU [*pleading with her urgently*]. You do not know what you are saying, child. Do you want to kill yourself? Listen. Do you not believe that you are subject to the Church of God on earth?

JOAN. Yes. When have I ever denied it?

LADVENU. Good. That means, does it not, that you are subject to our Lord the Pope, to the cardinals, the archbishops, and the bishops for whom his lordship stands here today?

JOAN. God must be served first.

D'ESTIVET. Then your voices command you not to submit yourself to the Church Militant?

JOAN. My voices do not tell me to disobey The Church; but God must be served first.

CAUCHON. And you, and not The Church, are to be the judge?

JOAN. What other judgment can I judge by but my own?

THE ASSESSORS [*scandalized*]. Oh! [*They cannot find words*].

CAUCHON: Out of your own mouth you have condemned yourself. (6, 136–38)

Notice that the last brief exchange between Cauchon and Joan is not in the court documents; there Joan does not say, "What other judgment can I judge by but my own," but rather, "I answer nothing from my own head." This is an important change, supporting Shaw's theory that Joan was in spirit a Protestant. Nevertheless, this passage in the play is Shaw's closest use of the trial records, and it indicates his determination to be faithful to Joan's personality.

Joan was especially appealing to Shaw because she was in many ways the sort of woman he admired and had in various guises already portrayed in his plays. As a purposeful young woman who enjoys taking charge—what Shaw called a born boss—she is the latest, and the youngest, in a long line of Shavian managerial women, going back to Blanche Sartorius of his first play, *Widowers' Houses*. She has the advantage over the others, for Shaw's purposes, of being unentangled by romance or the sexual interest of men. She cuts her hair short and wears soldier's outfits to lessen the awareness of her femininity—a sensible enough precaution—but the haircut and clothing emphasize her natural boyishness. She has, in this regard, some of the curious stage appeal of women characters disguised as males, a popular device in Elizabethan drama; but unlike, say, Shakespeare's Viola of *Twelfth Night*, whose essential femininity we are never allowed to forget, Joan is deliberately kept almost entirely sexless. The qualification is needed because Shaw does make deft use of her girlishness upon occasion, as when she bursts into tears of joy after the wind changes. And the poignancy of her loneliness in the final two scenes is intensified by our sense that this is a young woman being victimized by an assortment of powerful men.

Yet it is important to see Joan as a *youth,* rather than only a boyish female, in order to understand part of the deeper appeal she has for us. She possesses typical qualities of youth struggling against a world of adults—willfulness, brashness, impatience with customary procedures. The victories she wins before our eyes are not over the English troops—these triumphs we only hear about—but over her French elders, the establishment. In the first half of the work she is a fantasy figure: superkid, arriving from nowhere, saying in effect, "Take me to your leader—I will save you all!" She cuts down the self-important men of military and political and ecclesiastical eminence, and our pleasure in her triumphs is partly an oedipal one. The younger spectators in the audience can feel her to be a surrogate in their current conflict with their elders, and the older spectators can feel stirrings of their own buried rebellions against authority figures: in the darkened theater, with the make-believe enacted before us, we all become adolescents identifying with this fearless teenager.

But if Joan embodies an oedipal defiance of authority and seems for a time to be fulfilling the omnipotence fantasy of youth, she must finally pay a price proportional to the psychological and physical wounds inflicted on the multiform father. As the reality principle gains dominance in the last three scenes, we can accept the inevitability of her punishment more equably than that of a traditional tragic hero or heroine because we know from our own experience the retribution that follows upon the oedipal rebellion, in guilt if nothing else.

President Woodrow Wilson once said of men who acquire power that they either swell or grow; Joan, as she gains power, can certainly be said to grow. Her growth is visible by the fifth scene, when she is less girlish and naive. She is now aware of the wickedness of the world and realizes that no one at court will be sorry to see her return home—that many, in fact, will be glad to see her burnt. The innocent girl is turning into a disillusioned woman, and some of Shaw's finest touches lie in showing the coexistence of both phases in her. It is the adult who now says that her voices may be "only the echoes of my own commonsense" (5, 118), and who answers Dunois's charge of inconsistency in explaining her actions with the

retort "Well, I have to find reasons for you, because you do not believe in my voices. But the voices come first; and I find the reasons
after" (5, 111). She has shrewd things to say about warfare and the
futility of traditional methods of fighting, and she knows that her
bluntness in showing others their faults will antagonize them. Yet
in the same scene she can naively answer Charles's criticism that
she thinks she knows better than everyone else, "But I *do* know
better than any of you seem to. And I am not proud: I never speak
unless I know I am right" (5, 114). She also naively expects the
Archbishop to affirm in public that his earthly councils are "always
wrong" (5, 118).

Joan's increasing maturity continues to be displayed in the
final scene, but throughout the last scenes Shaw also has her ex-
hibit that swelling of the ego that Wilson said might result from
power. Her success in fighting now makes her feel free to give advice to kings and generals, and she declares to Dunois: "You don't
know how to begin a battle; and you don't know how to use your
cannons. And I do" (5, 115). She now speaks insultingly to that
very Archbishop of Rheims to whom she had humbly kneeled on
her first visit to court, and she frequently insults the churchmen at
the trial. She declares that her last word to all the clerics is that
"you are not fit that I should live among you" (6, 146).

Dunois accuses Joan of thinking "she has God in her pocket"
(5, 117), and she unwittingly substantiates this charge when she
brusquely orders the Archbishop to speak: "Then speak, you; and
tell [King Charles] that it is not God's will that he should take his
hand from the plough" but instead should go on fighting the English. The Archbishop rebukes her and specifies her flaw:

> If I am not so glib with the name of God as you are, it is because I
> interpret His will with the authority of The Church and of my sa-
> cred office. When you first came you respected it, and would not
> have dared to speak as you are now speaking. You came clothed
> with the virtue of humility; and because God blessed your enter-
> prises accordingly, you have stained yourself with the sin of pride.
> The old Greek tragedy is rising among us. It is the chastisement of
> hubris. (6, 113–14)

This, of course, makes the point, even too explicitly, and despite the sympathy we rightly feel for Joan at her trial, she does not

exactly invalidate the Archbishop's accusation. It may well be that with the prospect before her of being burned alive, all she can cling to is her conviction of righteousness, but her faith in herself and her voices has clearly been increased by her successes.

Yet pride is not hubris, and it is difficult to know how much the dramatist himself shared the Archbishop's view of Joan, how much he wanted his play to be comparable to a Greek tragedy. We recall that he termed the work, not a tragedy, but "A Chronicle Play in Six Scenes and an Epilogue." Although it is too purposively structured to be a chronicle play,[2] it is certainly not a tragedy either; for Shaw deliberately avoids the tragic mood in the epilogue and celebrates instead Joan's posthumous triumph. Nevertheless, I do think Shaw intended to exploit some elements of tragedy in the body of the play, including an element of pride in the fifth scene when Joan exhibits an impatient disdain for those who will not listen to her. He wanted her to have some human imperfections in order to keep the play in balance, to indicate that there is some justice in the charge of presumptuousness that is levied against her. But the deeper tragic current of the work has little to do with Joan's supposed hubris, and the Archbishop is not quite right in stating the matter in this way—it serves his convenience to do so.

Yes, Joan does display vanity. As she says at her trial, "Have I not been punished for my vanity? If I had not worn my cloth of gold surcoat in battle like a fool, that Burgundian soldier would never have pulled me backwards off my horse; and I should not have been here" (6, 136). She is proud of her military successes and impatient for Charles to press his advantage, but she has a right to be proud and she was right in her advice to Charles. Success has swelled her, but not as hugely as the Archbishop claims, and her pride is less for herself than for the power of God acting through her.

This is a critical point in judging her supposed hubris. Hubris is overweening pride, a defiance of the gods that allows one to think oneself immune to their powers, invulnerable. Thus, Oedipus haughtily boasts himself independent of the gods and their omens: what good were they, he asks, until he came along to solve the Sphinx's riddle? When he elatedly learns of the death of his supposed father, Polybos, he again mocks the divine oracles and their empty prophecies. The Chorus rightly warns of the outcome:

Haughtiness and the high hand of disdain
Tempt and outrage God's holy law;
And any mortal who dares hold
No immortal Power in awe
Will be caught up in a net of pain.[3]

Similarly, Hippolytus mocks the altar of Aphrodite and pays with his life. But Joan, far from defying the supernatural forces, insists on her servitude to God and His messengers. She is awed by the immortal power who sends His saints to her. In the name of God, she denies the churchmen's claim that they alone can mediate God's word. She has some vanity and is somewhat puffed up with her successes; she could be more tactful and mannerly. But her real pride is in serving God and treasuring the successes He has brought her. The Greek play most pertinent to her dilemma is *Antigone,* for the heroine of that work also defies earthly powers in order to obey religious obligations, and she shows firmness rather than excessive pride. Joan's fundamental "sin," according to the churchmen at the trial, is not hubris but heresy. They see her as doctrinally defying the church—its authority and instructions. She sees herself as obeying supreme religious imperatives.

Indeed, it is Joan's humility that she must guard against. William Searle rightly says that "she is tempted through her humility rather than through her pride."[4] From Baudricourt at the beginning to Cauchon at the end, Joan is told that her secular goals are mistaken and should be humbly renounced. Only the proud certainty that she is on a divine mission sustains her through her trials. Her death results, as Louis Crompton remarks, from her virtues and not her defects.[5]

Even the Inquisitor is ready to grant that Joan's truest excesses are not those of pride but of piety. She is nonetheless a dangerous heretic. Ladvenu, the compassionate young Dominican, is so drawn to Joan's goodness as to wonder aloud whether there is "any great harm in this girl's heresy?" "Is it not," he asks, "merely her simplicity?" The questions draw forth the longest speech in the play, the Inquisitor's closely reasoned reply. Heresy, as he tells us, at first seems innocent and even laudable, its expositors often superior to their neighbors in gentleness and piety. Joan's "excesses have been the excesses of religion and charity and not of worldliness and wantoness." But heresy, apparently harmless and even

lovable in its beginnings, ends with "a monstrous horror of unnatu-
ral wickedness" (6, 130)—ends, as Cauchon has said earlier, in a
world "wracked back into barbarism" (4, 103).

The clash between Joan and the Church is thus nonnegotiable.
If she alone has the right to judge the authenticity of her voices and
of God's messages, then the Church's authority and function are
undermined. She ultimately represents for Shaw the principle of
Christianity without a Church, or of a Church reserved for only
secondary, social purposes. In her relationship to God, she is willing to bypass ecclesiastical institutions and to set up her own
communion. As is said of her in the epilogue: "The girls in the field
praise thee; for thou hast raised their eyes; and they see that there
is nothing between them and heaven" (165). Every man in the end
becomes his own priest.

Shaw thus sees Joan as quintessentially Protestant—"the first
Protestant saint and martyr," as he called her in a letter to his
friend Father Joseph Leonard. But if so, how could the Catholic
Church have canonized her? Shaw asked the reverend to clarify
this puzzling matter; his letter to Father Leonard indicates how well
formulated Shaw's thoughts on Joan were even four months before
he began his first draft of the play:

11th December 1922

Dear Father Leonard

. . . I always forget to ask you about a historical question in which
I am interested. It is about Joan of Arc. Joan was the first Nation-
alist and the first Protestant. In the latter capacity she was tried
by the Inquisition—quite mercifully and fairly, all things considered—and as she insisted on convicting herself out of her own
mouth every time she opened it, she was condemned as a heretic,
which she was. She recanted; relapsed; and was then handed
over to the secular arm, which, being English, burnt her offhand
without waiting for the necessary secular trial.

This left the king in the very uncomfortable position of having
been crowned by a heretic and sorceress. Accordingly, when the
English were driven out and the king firmly established, Joan's
relatives moved the courts for a revision of the verdict and a lifting
of the interdict. There was a retrial which was an orgy of good-
natured perjury. Her old judges were dead or indisposed to offend

the court and incur unpopularity by opposing the relatives; and Joan was rehabilitated with enthusiasm.

In 1907 (I think) she was canonized. Where can I find a record of the proceedings? What I want to know is how the Church got over the fact, which must have been raised by the advocatus diaboli if he did his duty to his client that Joan asserted a right of private judgment as against the Church. St Clare and St Francis did the same virtually; but Joan did it explicitly, and was excommunicated for it. Luther or Carson could have done no more: she was the first Protestant saint and martyr. The sorcery could be got over, as the Church recognizes celestial visions and can hold that the Inquisitors were wrong in deciding that Joan's visions were temptations by the devil.

I may write a play about her some day; and this is the only point on which I do not feel fully equipped. If you cannot answer offhand, you might set the College discussing it for me.[6]

Father Leonard answered the dramatist by claiming in effect that Joan's private judgment was not exercised against the Church, since only "in the loosest way of speaking" was the Inquisition at all involved. The trial was conducted by a "local ecclesiastical court presided over by Cauchon . . . without any reference to the Pope and indeed carried out in defiance of [Joan's] appeal to the head of the Church. Her conviction then by that local tribunal in no way bound the Roman authorities." Moreover, rather than the trial being merciful and just, it was "illegal and unjust. Cauchon was clearly out for her death" (*CL*, 3:797).

Appreciative as Shaw was of Father Leonard's arguments, he did not accept them, and both in the play and the preface he insists on the legitimacy of the trial and on Cauchon's fairness. He repeats his claim that Joan had exercised her private judgment against the authority of the Church and was therefore a Protestant martyr. As he delicately phrases it in the preface, "her canonization was a magnificently Catholic gesture as the canonization of a Protestant saint by the Church of Rome" (37).

7

The Issue

By trusting her private judgment rather than ecclesiastical and secular authorities, by embodying for the dramatist the new currents of Protestantism and nationalism, Shaw's Joan represents the spirit of individualism and change. The opposition she arouses and the fate she suffers are the price often paid by those who would alter mankind's condition. Without such people, the reformers, the self-selected saints, as Shaw calls them, societies cannot evolve.

Yet our initial sympathy for the rebel and the innovator, for those who defy the establishment and its ways, may fade when we consider those persons who publicly burn school books that teach evolution, or who refuse to pay taxes until the government pursues a foreign policy they advocate, or who defy the state's order to inoculate their children against disease because they oppose the use of medicine, or who vandalize abortion clinics, or who explode bombs on crowded streets to advance a political cause. These are only a few examples of the innumerable self-appointed saints with nostrums for curing what they perceive to be society's ills and who must be forcibly restrained from action. Some claim to hear voices and instructions from supernatural beings; many a killer has claimed to be obeying God's commands. "What will the world be like when [mankind]'s accumulated wisdom and knowledge and experience . . . are thrust into the kennel by every ignorant laborer or dairymaid whom the devil can puff up with the monstrous self-conceit of being directly inspired from heaven? It will be a world of blood, of fury, of devastation, of each man striving for his own hand: in the end a world wrecked back into barbarism" (4, 103).

Cauchon's words have power and truth even when we replace the word *mankind* (which I substituted) with the original words "The Church." Throughout the world we find chaos reigning in places where self-appointed saviors seek to impose their will on society for its own good. If life is not to be, as Hobbes put it, nasty, brutish, and short, societies must enforce laws preventing people from acting any way they think fit. "The government of the world, political, industrial, and domestic," Shaw states in the preface, "has to be carried on mostly by the giving and obeying of orders" (43), and "we may prate of toleration as we will, but society must always draw a line somewhere between allowable conduct and insanity or crime, in spite of the risk of mistaking sages for lunatics and saviors for blasphemers. We must persecute, even to the death" (41).

How, then, are we to deal with the question raised by Joan's voices and visions, with her conviction that she was divinely inspired? After all, even during the mere 13 months of her activity, Joan was not the only woman thereabouts to claim she was receiving instructions from heaven. A certain Catherine de la Rochelle was a rival visionary, claiming guidance from a celestial white lady dressed in gold who advised her on ways to raise money for the Dauphin and ways he might make peace with the Duke of Burgundy. Joan spent two successive nights with Catherine waiting for the white lady to put in an appearance, but to no avail (Murray, 52–53). Yet if she could not see Catherine's vision, neither could Catherine see Joan's—nobody but Joan ever heard her voices or shared her sight of Saint Margaret or Saint Michael. How is one to judge between competing claimants to God's word?

A seeming solution, which Shaw accepted, is the pragmatic one. The claimant is to be judged by the consequences of the "inspiration." Catherine de la Rochelle's advice was apparently not as sound as Joan's. As Dunois tells Joan, it is her sensible reasons, not her voices, that promote his confidence in her. As a result of the advice Joan's voices give her, she breaks the English siege of Orléans, wins other victories, and consecrates the king. "I have brought them luck and victory," she says to Dunois. "I have set them right when they were doing all sorts of stupid things: I have crowned Charles and made him a real king" (5, 109–10). As Shaw says of her, "Her policy was also quite sound . . . [her actions] were military and political masterstrokes that saved France" (P, 12–13).

Furthermore, "she objected to foreigners on the sensible ground that they were not in their proper place in France" (P, 23); the nationalism and Protestantism she represented were both, Shaw maintains, part of the necessary forward movement of western civilization. In sum, Joan was an agent of what Shaw called the Life Force; she was a selfless servant of the "evolutionary appetite," a woman to be judged by what she accomplished.

Can this satisfy us? Perhaps. But a critic of Shaw could nonetheless make a strong argument against his position. Such a critic would say that Joan's sensible and quite sound policies certainly did not seem so to many churchmen, for the reasons powerfully stated by Cauchon and the Inquisitor in the play. And in historical reality, learned theologians of the University of Paris found her actions ungodly and anti-Christian, stating in a letter of July 1430 that she perpetrated offenses "against our very gentle Creator, His Faith, and His Holy Church."[1] Nor, for that matter, did her policies seem sensible and quite sound to the English and their Burgundian allies. Charles's political prospects were desperate before Joan arrived; that desperation was probably the chief reason he was willing to believe her claim that God had sent her to help him, and the chief reason he entrusted her with an army. Yet without her, there might have been an end of bloodshed. "She disrupted all possibility of real peace by reviving a languishing war," as the English king phrased it in a letter of June 1431 (Rankin, 55). And the king's chief ally, Philip the Good, Duke of Burgundy, was overjoyed by her capture, exclaiming in a letter of May 1430:

> It has pleased our Blessed Creator to allow and grant us a great grace—*The Maid* has been captured! Other captains, knights, squires, and soldiers with her were taken or drowned or killed, their names at this hour we do not yet know. Thank God none of our followers nor any of the followers of the King are killed or taken, and only twenty are wounded. This capture, we truly believe, will be welcome news everywhere. Now the error and foolish belief of those who approved and favored this woman will be recognized. We write you this news in the hope that it will give you joy, comfort, and satisfaction, and that you will thank and praise our Creator Who sees and knows all things. (Rankin, 99–100)

Charles VII, who owed his crown to Joan, eventually defeated his enemies. Yet one cannot say for certain that France benefited by having Charles as king. Perhaps the country would have been better off had its national unity been delayed until the nineteenth century, as was Italy's and Germany's. Certain regions of France—Guyenne, for example—were far worse off after Charles finally drove out the English, as J. M. Robertson pointed out in his learned critical study of Shaw's historiography (55). It is not inconceivable, albeit unlikely, that England and France could have become one country of composite population, with different linguistic heritages, as is Canada or Belgium or Spain or Great Britain itself. Democracy in France might have been advanced by such an arrangement; the revolution of 1789 and the European slaughterhouse created by Napoléon might have been avoided. American history itself, in that the United States was considerably influenced by the rivalry between England and France, would have been immeasurably different and perhaps less bloody. It is historical determinism (and Shaw was a Marxist in this regard) to hold that Europe had to evolve exactly as it did and to go through the stages of nationalism and Protestantism. To credit every major change to the Life Force and an evolutionary appetite is to abandon all criteria for judging changes. When is evolution not devolution? Shaw himself excoriated many of the changes taking place in his own lifetime, changes that their proponents found desirable. He also accepted (unlike many of the Fabians) the need for imperialism—defending it as early as the Boer War in 1898 and as late as Italy's invasion of Ethiopia in 1936. He did not in principle object, as he says Joan did, to troops being on foreign soil, though in particular instances, as in his native Ireland, he did object. At any rate, the case against Joan was in part based on what her enemies regarded as a senseless prolonging of a bloody war. For example, Article 18 of the Accusation against her reads as follows:

> So long as Jeanne remained with Charles, she did dissuade him with all her power, him and those with him, from consenting to any treaty of peace, any arrangement with his adversaries; inciting them always to murder and effusion of blood; affirming that they could only have peace by sword and lance; and that God willed it so, because otherwise the enemies of the king would not give up that which they held in his kingdom; to fight them thus, is, she told them, one of the greatest benefits that can happen to all Christendom. (Murray, 348)

How can this self-designated agent of God have had true piety if she brought hatred and slaughter?

The English, as we learn from the account in Holinshed's *Chronicles,* regarded Joan as a "miraclemonger" with a "murtherous mind" who kept the war going by her "deadlie mischiefe" for two years without any attempt at making peace. She was a "damnable sorcerer suborned by satan," rightly burnt "for witchcraft and sorcerie."[2] It was from this hostile perspective that Shakespeare developed the portrait of her we find in *Henry VI, Part I.*

What were the signs that Joan's voices were heaven-sent? This was asked at her actual trial. The Church accepts that God can deliver inspirations to selected individuals through saints and archangels, but some signs are needed to verify that these are indeed God's inspirations. Joan's "signs" were her victories, but for the English and their Burgundian and ecclesiastical sympathizers in France, these victories were defeats. The divine miracles of one side were the devilish disasters of the other. The English ruling family was far more pious than was Charles's, and therefore could only feel themselves more deserving of God's favor. For Joan to beat the English could only mean that she was guided by the Devil—"a disciple and limb of the Fiend," as the Duke of Bedford called her (Rankin, 68). In an age that believed unquestioningly in witchcraft, she was, for the English, manifestly a witch—and witches should be burned.

Observing Shaw's play, we do not at all feel this way. We are made sympathetic to Joan, seeing things predominantly though not exclusively from her viewpoint. But we must remember that multitudes of people at the time regarded her actions as dreadful. And unless there is general agreement on the beneficial consequences of an individual's actions, the pragmatic test for judging the divinity of the inspiration is of dubious value. Indeed, according to a passage of Shaw's written less than a decade earlier, in *Common Sense about the War,* even Joan's Christianity may be, by implication, open to question, for in the name of Christ she encouraged bloody warfare. A bishop is no longer a true Christian when he, "at the first shot abandons the worship of Christ and rallies his flock round the altar of Mars"; we should "close our professedly Christian Churches the moment war is declared by us, and reopen them only on the signing of the treaty of peace" (*CW,* 21:100).

It is not, of course, to catch Shaw up in contradictions that we remind ourselves of the case that can be made against Joan. It is, precisely, to reveal the truth of Shaw's statement in the preface that the more closely we grapple with the issue, the more difficult it becomes (39). A few years after *Saint Joan* had been written, a Quaker correspondent of Shaw's, J. E. Whiting, argued with the dramatist about Charlotte Corday. Whiting strongly defended her action in stabbing to death Marat, who was persecuting her party, the Girondists, and he compared her to Joan: "Charlotte, like Joan, was a pureminded high souled young woman, who was inspired by the troubles of her country to offer herself a willing sacrifice in an endeavor to save it from destruction. In her case death was certain, though to Joan remained strong hope of survival. As for the killing, the one did it in combination, and called it 'War,' the other individually, and it is called 'Assassination.' . . . All honour both to her and to Joan." Shaw protested that he could not really associate Charlotte Corday with Joan, because she had "murderous rancor," and especially because her actions ended up hurting the Girondists more (*CL*, 4:56–57). But would the comparison have been valid if she had helped her party? Is the test, again, the pragmatic one of success in eliminating a personal or political enemy? The issue remained as thorny for Shaw as it continues to be for us.

Prestige in our culture attaches to newness and individuality and youthfulness. We accept glumly the claims of tradition and societal regulation. But in practice we often deplore the presumption of ignorant and inexperienced youth—think of your insolent younger brother or sister or cousin or friend—and we defend tested and proven practices and institutions. We would not tolerate for long any 18-year-old acquaintance who not only told us what we should do but insisted that God was using her as a messenger to tell us what to do. Her individualistic judgments may trample on the rights of our group, and in following her inner light she may blow out the communal light that guides us. We are, after all, the beneficiaries of that society—that social order—she would change simply because she *knows* she knows what is good for us.

How much tolerance can society give to people like this who flout its fundamental tenets and thereby threaten its very existence? The cluster of ideational conflicts the play presents—change versus order, the individual versus society, inspiration versus law—can be lucidly discussed, but particular instances immediately tangle us in confusion. What do we do with a group of intensely religious terrorists who use modern weapons to promote their cause, a cause for which we may even have sympathy? Do we kill them as they have killed others? Do we imprison them for life? Do we let them go free because they selflessly serve what they regard as noble and divine ends? Is taking up arms for a private cause ever justified? Should we ever defy a law we feel is outrageously unjust? Such are the questions that properly arise from *Saint Joan* and that establish its continuing power and relevance.

Shaw himself was pulled in opposite directions in trying to answer these questions, and he dramatized the tensions of this conflict in the play. It was, as we shall see in a later chapter, a very personal conflict. Here it suffices to note the sound sense and right principles on *both* sides of the conflict: we need change, and we need order. The churchmen in the play are quite as dedicated to the public good as is Joan. They know the dangers to social stability created by a self-appointed martyr; they know also the danger to the martyr's own soul in perhaps coming to think, as Dunois says of Joan, that "she has God in her pocket." The play shows the clash, not of good and evil, but of opposing goods. And the same clash will continue to exist as long as people want the benefits of order as well as change, of community cohesion as well as individual initiative.

8

The Epilogue Mystery

Thus far we have found all sorts of virtues in Shaw's drama—in its structure, its characterization, its important ideas. But *Saint Joan* is not a faultless work. It is too ambitious; it takes too many risks. For one thing, Shaw pours ideas into his play with such zest that they spill over. Warwick and Cauchon are given too much to say in the tent scene, as is the Inquisitor in his tirade in the last scene. (Shaw later indicated how the speeches of all three men could be pruned in his filmscript of the work.) Furthermore, in that tent scene we also endure the overclever anachronistic use of the terms *nationalism* and *Protestantism* as well as the excessive historical prescience of the speakers, a prescience Shaw unconvincingly defends in the preface (51–52). Again, the excited ending of scene 3 is both rushed and emotionally forced. And finally, Shaw's attempt to suggest Joan's peasant background by giving her English north-country speech sometimes produces awkwardness, as does his giving her Ann Whitefield's belittling trick of first-naming and nick-naming the men, especially her use of "Charlie" for the Dauphin.

Yet all these are minor blemishes, the price we readily pay and overlook to concentrate on the work's massive virtues. Only in the lengthy epilogue, a semicomic fantasy differing in mood from the final scenes, do we encounter a doubtful section that cannot be passed over lightly, a section that has aroused a good deal of controversy. Some commentators, such as Desmond MacCarthy (171) and Edmund Wilson, regard the epilogue as essential to the play, serving to clarify the play's issues. "I do not see," Wilson writes, "how those critics who have objected to the Epilogue can

really understand what the play is about: if the Epilogue were to go,
the tent scene would have to go, too—as would also the Inquisitor's
speech and a great deal more; we should have to have a different
play built on different lines, and with Joan's individual tragedy and
not human history as its theme."[1] Other critics, such as James
Agate (70) and A. N. Kaul, find the epilogue superfluous and even
damaging. Kaul expresses his objection as follows:

> With its fantasy tableaux, its flip jokes, its common soldier (on a
> day's parole from hell) railing against "kings and captains and
> bishops" and telling Joan that she has "as good a right to your
> notions as they have to theirs'—even with Joan's famous last cry:
> "How long, O Lord, how long?"—the Epilogue mostly brings back
> the Shaw so admirably absent from the play itself. It is Shaw's
> theme bereft of the historical sanction of its own time, and one is
> struck though not surprised by the uncertainties of tone and in-
> tellectual argument alike that accompany the shifting of the
> mental perspective to the present period.[2]

This division among the critics is duplicated among the actresses who have performed the leading role. Sybil Thorndike, for
whom the part of Joan was written, regarded the epilogue as a very
"necessary part of the shape" of the work (Mander, 14). Welsh actress Sian Phillips enjoyed the epilogue: "It's such a relaxed thing to
do, so good-humored."[3] American actress Joyce Ebert acknowledged that the epilogue "is hard to play after you've been burned at
the stake, but I like it. Joan is bouncier, more positive, more for-
giving . . . less intense" (Hill, 149). Among those who had reservations, Uta Hagan thought it the most difficult scene in the play
(Hill, 44) and Lee Grant was bothered enormously by it—"I never
got over the epilogue" (Hill, 149). Janet Suzman remembers
"fighting about it because at a certain time in rehearsal, I thought,
'Enough! The story is told. We don't need the coda' " (Hill, 159).

Shaw answered the early critics of the epilogue by stating in
the preface that he could not imply that "Joan's history in the world
ended unhappily with her execution." He felt "it was necessary by
hook or crook to shew the canonized Joan as well as the inciner-
ated one" (53). And in a program note to the first London production, Shaw advised the audience that without the epilogue, "the
play would be only a sensational tale of a girl who was burnt, leav-

ing the spectators plunged in horror, despairing of humanity. The true tale of Saint Joan is a tale with a glorious ending; and any play that did not make this clear would be an insult to her memory" (Laurence, 213).

As in all controversial matters of art, each of us has the pleasure of making his or her own decision. My own opinion is somewhat ambivalent, though on balance I am sorry this particular epilogue was written. One can easily conceive of a much shorter and traditional epilogue—spoken, say, by Charles or Dunois or even Warwick. It would tell of the 1456 rehabilitation decision, which found Joan innocent and the trial fraudulent; and the speaker might then wonder whether the Church would ever go so far as to canonize her. Such a straightforward or perhaps ironically edged epilogue (with a program note stating that Joan was canonized in 1920) would fully meet Edmund Wilson's requirement that Shaw's study of the forces of human history be completed, and it would fulfill Shaw's desire that the audience know of Joan's "glorious ending." In a word, we need not have had an epilogue that is longer than most of the scenes in the play and disruptive of the serious and touching mood the play has achieved.

Admittedly, the epilogue we do have is in many respects a masterly little theater piece. Its quasisurrealistic stage effects are resourceful, particularly its use of lighting; and the dramatist smoothly brings on and then removes his several characters. Some of the talk is mildly amusing and, best of all, Joan is given a powerful moment at the end. Bathed in white radiance, as the bells of midnight sound, she intones her subsequently famous words: "Oh God that madest this beautiful earth, when will it be ready to receive Thy saints? How long, O Lord, how long?"

Yet some of the stage effects are gimmicky (such as the visions of Joan's statues at Winchester and Rheims cathedrals) and the handling of most of the characters mechanical and diminishing. Shaw converts them into a mere chorus and thereby reduces their distinctiveness and humanity. Maurice Valency has rightly condemned the "truly wretched litany" that the principal characters address to the saint,[4] and I find not only the manner but the matter of the litany puzzling. For the epilogue regrettably changes as well as simplifies the meanings of the play. All of Shaw's skill in building up the case for Cauchon and the Inquisitor, of keeping their side of the argument powerful, is now wasted. The Archbishop attacks himself for worldliness, the Inquisitor declares the law to have been blind, Cauchon wonders whether a Christ must perish in every age.

Furthermore, melodramatic contrasts reappear and undermine the tragic dilemmas of the play. A good is no longer in conflict with another good. Now we learn that Joan was destroyed by foolish, shortsighted men. The once subtle defender of the necessary mediating role of the Church kneels to Joan and simplemindedly (and for a Catholic priest, implausibly) declares that "the girls in the field praise thee; for thou hast raised their eyes; and they see that there is nothing between them and heaven" (165). Rhetoric replaces reasoning: "The Church Militant sent this woman to the fire," Cauchon declares, "but even as she burned, the flames whitened into the radiance of the Church Triumphant" (158). A symptom of Shaw's strange disregard of his play is that he took an epilogue line he had originally written for Joan (Tyson, 74) but, deciding it was too boastful, gave it inappropriately to Cauchon: "Must then a Christ perish in torment in every generation to save those that have no imagination" (161). Cauchon's "imagination" in the play is not at all defective: he imagines quite vividly the consequences of allowing heresies like Joan's to go uncurbed. Cauchon is not only different in the epilogue from in the play but also inconsistent within the epilogue itself—at first self-justifying and then repentant without cause.

This points to Shaw's own dilemma and inconsistency, which he avoids in the play but cannot avoid when he deals with later events. In the play Shaw strives to make Joan's 1431 trial fair and lawful and even merciful. But the 1456 Sentence of Rehabilitation found the trial unfair and unlawful and unmerciful—"full of cozenage, iniquity, inconsequences, and manifest errors, in fact as well as in law," to use the exact words of the judges and high church officials (Murray, 326). If that judgment were correct, Shaw's play was wrong. Thus Shaw, to preserve his play, had to declare the Sentence of Rehabilitation wrong. This he boldly proceeds to do in the epilogue through the mouth of Ladvenu, who states: "At this [Rehabilitation] inquiry from which I have just come, there was shameless perjury, courtly corruption, calumny of the dead who did their duty according to their lights, cowardly evasion of the issue, testimony made of idle tales that could not impose on a ploughboy"

(153). The proceedings were "an insult to justice," and "an orgy of lying and foolishness." Shaw seems outraged indeed that the Rehabilitation judgment refuses to fit his theory. Yet unless that judgment is accepted, Joan cannot be absolved and her future canonization by the Church will not occur. What, then, can Shaw do? He can (and does) seek refuge in metaphor, rhetoric, and paradox. Ladvenu ends his denunciation of the Sentence of Rehabilitation by declaring that out of this "orgy of lying and foolishness, the truth is set in the noonday sun on the hilltop; the white robe of innocence is cleansed from the smirch of the burning faggots; the holy life is sanctified; the true heart that lived through the flame is consecrated; a great lie is silenced for ever; and a great wrong is set right before all men" (153). What great lie and what great wrong? If the first trial was valid for Shaw—"not only honest and legal, but exceptionally merciful in respect of sparing Joan the torture which was customary," as the preface puts it (33)—then there was neither lie nor wrong.

The epilogue contains another disturbing contradiction. Shaw seems to have Joan more than reconciled to her death, since it heightened her fame. As the Irish critic Nicholas Grene has said, "The Epilogue is antitragic in that it allows us to escape the finality of death, so fundamental to the sense of tragedy, into a realm of cosy immortality."[5] And as the English actress Joan Plowright has observed, the epilogue is very hard to play because "if you're not careful, you can come on very self-satisfied and complacent and just beam at all those people around the bed" (Hill, 112). Moreover, Joan feels that her martyrdom served a *useful* purpose. As she says to Cauchon: "I hope men will be the better for remembering me; and they would not remember me so well if you had not burned me" (157). And when Chaplain de Stogumber declares he was redeemed from his cruel ways by the sight of the Maid burning at the stake, Joan says, truly even if wryly, "Well, if I saved all those he would have been cruel to if he had not been cruel to me, I was not burnt for nothing, was I?" (162). If in its consequences, then, Joan's death seems justified to Shaw, in retrospect we were wrong to be so affected by the final scene of the play. And if martyrs serve a useful purpose, they should not be denied their martyrdom. Saints should *not* be welcomed by the world as Joan asks the world to do in her final rhetorical flourish. The world should never be ready to receive its saints if the price of that receptivity will be the saints' lessened influence. A world truly ready to receive its saints would not need them.

The epilogue is thus discordant with the play not only in its style but also in its content. It contains confusions and inconsistencies that are absent in the play. It seems to resurrect Joan and to give such accolades to her fame that the agony of her final moments—the deliberate burning to death of a 19-year-old girl—becomes distant. Shaw did not, after all, believe that Joan was going to heaven after her death. Hence it might seem a little callous of the 67-year-old dramatist to put the stress on what he calls her "glorious ending" through sainthood when we cannot know whether she herself would have traded her life to have the word *saint* put posthumously in front of her name.

We are really left with the mystery of why Shaw wrote this particular epilogue at all. His own justification for it is unconvincing, for the play proper does not leave the spectators plunged in horror, despairing of humanity. Rather, the play implies that Joan's history did not end with her burning. Shaw takes pains to have Ladvenu remark after the execution that Joan's story may have just begun. And Warwick also doubts that the last has been heard of her. Since Shaw's contemporary audience had heard a great deal of Joan's canonization only four years before the play was produced, there certainly was no need to inform them of it in an epilogue; and if the playwright felt that latter-day audiences would truly not know of it, a single-line program note would have informed them that Joan was rehabilitated in 1456 and canonized in 1920. At most, a dozen or so lines of traditional epilogue could have conveyed the essentials of Joan's "glorious ending."

Perhaps one possible answer to the mystery of the epilogue's composition is that Shaw had conceived it before the play. To his friend Mrs. Campbell he had written from Orléans in September 1913:

> I have been all over the Joan of Arc country. How they canonize her you may see from the previous postcard. I shall do a Joan play some day, beginning with the sweeping up of the cinders and orange peel after her martyrdom, and going on with Joan's arrival in Heaven. I should have God about to damn the English for their share in her betrayal and Joan producing an end of burnt stick in

70

arrest of Judgment. "What's that? Is it one of the faggots?" says God. "No," says Joan, "it's what is left of the two sticks a common English soldier tied together and gave me as I went to the stake; for they wouldn't even give me a crucifix; and you cannot damn the common people of England, represented by that soldier because a poor cowardly riff raff of barons and bishops were too futile to resist the devil." (*CL*, 3, 201–2)

And he joked that one of the scenes would include such earlier Joan detractors as Voltaire and Shakespeare "running down bye streets in heaven to avoid meeting Joan." It may be that Shaw thought out other aspects of the epilogue long before he turned his mind to the play proper. Perhaps it was a fondness for this material that determined him to use it.

His decision may also have been guided by uneasiness with the tragic mood at the end of the play. Shaw was a writer of comedy and his dominant bent was toward it. Moreover, he had peculiar difficulty in accepting the gravity of death. He was notorious for rushing about at the conclusion of funerals, trying to cheer people up with jokes; he even made the joke after his own mother's cremation that she had now become like Cinderella. Lewis Casson, the director of the first London performance of *Saint Joan*, noted that Shaw wanted the epilogue to be almost farcical when the play was in rehearsal: "He so overemphasized this with overplaying and funny business, that although [the actor] Ernest Thesiger and I induced him to modify this considerably at rehearsal, it still shocked the audience far more than was necessary and marred the essential beauty of the play's design" (Mander, 18).

There are other possible answers to the mystery of the epilogue—and of course several motives may have combined toward the same end. In the "dream" epilogue Shaw was least bound by history or by the historical Joan and could create more freely than elsewhere in the play. He may have wanted to reward himself, as it were, after having stayed closer to his sources than in any of his other historical dramas. He may even have wanted an opportunity to tip the scales strongly in Joan's favor out of an authorial guilt, for in the play itself he strives peculiarly hard to be fairer to the Church than he knew the proceedings justified. And finally, he may have wanted to tip the scales out of a personal guilt. These last two points are addressed in the concluding chapters of this volume.

9

The Playwright as Historian

Shaw was unusually modest in responding to the praise heaped on *Saint Joan*. "It is the easiest play I have ever had to write," he said. "All I've done is to put down the facts, to arrange Joan for the stage. The trial scene is merely a report of the actual trial. I have used Joan's very words: thus she spoke, thus she behaved" (Pearson, 342). This modest assertion of historical fidelity is in large measure accurate. Information about Joan's life is abundant, due to the records of the 1431 trial and the 1456 rehabilitation proceedings; and the drama of her sudden rise, her heroic achievements, and her dreadful death inheres in the data. Yet these documents, available to other writers, too, never generated a theatrical work remotely like Shaw's. Of the scores of plays about Joan, his is unique and justifiably the most famous. Thus "to put down the facts" actually involved, as we have seen earlier, an extremely skillful and inventive hand.

How inventive? How much, that is, did Shaw embellish the story? How much did he add to and omit from the documentary characterizations of Joan and the other principal figures? How faithful was he to the inner meaning of the events and the spirit of the times? Can we take leave of the play with a sense of having been exposed not only to a powerful drama but also to the true history of this celebrated woman?

In writing the play, the challenge of truthfulness was greater than we might at first expect. Even allowing himself the scope of a long play (with a running time of three and a half hours), Shaw had to leave out most of the events of Joan's life—her early years and family life, the several battles in which she took part, her dealings with the ordinary French folk who increasingly worshiped her, her capture and subsequent attempt to escape, and the many months of her imprisonment. (These alone could have supplied material for several plays.) The exigencies of stage time required much compression. Joan's three trips to Baudricourt and her two to the Dauphin are condensed to one trip to each, and the final scene coalesces two separate trials. Men who swarm across the pages of the documents are trimmed down to the handful of characters who people the play. A short letter by the Archbishop of Rheims serves as the few bones on which the dramatist fleshes out a complete character. A statement that an English assistant to the Bishop of Winchester called a French Bishop a traitor, when it seemed Joan would not go to the stake, was all that history provided for the creation of John de Stogumber.

Depicting Joan herself was undoubtedly the greatest challenge of all, and only partly because here the historical material was almost too detailed. People who have loomed large on the world's stage tend to shrink when carried directly on to the theater's stage. Their well-defined features inhibit the writer's imagination and turn him into a humble copyist, unlikely to capture the charisma of the original. Even Shakespeare is not able to give quite as much fullness of life to his English kings as to his more legendary rulers such as Lear and Macbeth. Shaw's own Napoléon and his Empress Catherine have less living presence than the imagined Candida, say, or Mrs. Warren, or Major Barbara, or a dozen other created characters from his plays. (Shaw's best early historical figure, Caesar, is as much a created as a found character.) Moreover, Joan was a highly virtuous individual, and such people, whether invented or real, are notoriously hard to make convincing. And beyond this, Joan was so inherently improbable a person—shrewd and naive, earthy and pious, overbearing and gentle, serious and cheerful—that she would have given pause to the most self-confident dramatist. And as if this were not challenge enough, Joan also came attended by her voices and miracles, and these improbabilities in one form or other had to be included.

How, then, does Shaw fare as a truth-teller about this woman and her time? In answering this, we should keep in mind two distinctions. First, the Joan of the preface is not exactly the same as the Joan of the play. In the former, Shaw makes claims for her—for her intellectuality, her advocacy of rational dress for women, her service to the Life Force—that are not argued in the play and hence constitute a separate and far less important historical issue. We must further distinguish between Joan's personality and her views. On the key question of Joan's personality in the play, a historian such as the distinguished medievalist Johan Huizinga gives Shaw full credit for the portrait of Joan: "Shaw has seen the basic contours of that essence [of her being] lucidly, and has portrayed them clearly."[1] The traits she displays in the play are also visible from the records. Huizinga would only have liked her to be shown as somewhat more heroic and also more feminine. Another historian, J. Van Kan, would have preferred her earlier speeches to be less naive and awkward.[2] But in the main these specialists find that Shaw's Joan mirrors the historical figure, and my own reading of the records leaves me astonished at Shaw's deftness in selecting and conveying so many facets of her personality.

It should be mentioned, however, that some commentators find Shaw's portrait quite wide of the mark. T. S. Eliot, as we have seen, accused Shaw of sacrilegiously turning her from a saint into "a great middle-class reformer" (Evans, 294); Norwegian scholar Ingvald Raknem thought that she had been distorted into a boastful, unwomanly, and vulgar girl.[3] Raknem's opinions, admittedly, can find support in a few of Joan's lines but by no means in the majority of them, and an able actress can by intonation and manner take the edge off even the occasional boast and vulgarity.

A conjectural side issue is whether Shaw used any contemporary models in his portrait of the Maid. Stanley Weintraub makes a characteristically barbarous assertion that Shaw had none other than Lawrence of Arabia as his model,[4] but that absurdity has been charitably ignored by most Shaw critics. A far more sensible possibility, explored by Brian Tyson (17–19), is that Shaw may occasionally have thought of his Fabian friend Mary Hankinson, a strong, athletic, and religious woman who for many years managed the Fabian summer schools. Shaw inscribed her gift copy of *Saint Joan* with the words: "To Mary Hankinson, the only woman I know who does not believe she was the model for Joan and also the only woman who actually was" (*CL*, 3:554). The second clause is possibly a little less extravagant than the first, and allowance has to be made for Shaw's usual Irish gallantry; but it may be that recollections of Mary Hankinson, with her "school-boy heart and skipper air," as one admirer put it, helped to flesh out the impressions Shaw formed from the trial records. But above all, the dramatist wrote the part for an actress he greatly admired, Sybil Thorndike, whom in late 1922 he had seen play Beatrice in Shelley's *The Cenci* and whose performance in the trial scene much impressed him. With the abundance of documentary descriptions of Joan's personality and of her own words before him, and with an actress he could tailor the part for, Shaw had little need for more remote models.

On the historicity of Joan's outlook, Shaw has received rather less commendation than on his rendering of her character. Huizinga believes the dramatist is accurate in showing Joan as not mystical and not a spiritual ecstatic—"all visionary terminology of the usual sort is utterly alien to her"—and he praises Shaw for strongly opposing the idea that labeling Joan's voices a morbid symptom is enough to define their significance. The form in which Joan conceived of her celestial advisors, Huizinga states, "is bound to the conceptual world in which she lived. It was just as natural and logical for her to visualize the voices as saints and angels as it is for a modern man to borrow his terms from the concepts of physics" (223). But Van Kan maintains that the play's greatest lapse from history lies in having Joan herself offer at times a naturalistic explanation for her voices. When she agrees with Baudricourt that her voices come from her imagination, because, as she says, "that is how the messages of God come to me," it is Shaw and not Joan who speaks. Joan believed her voices to be the actual voices of saints dwelling in another world, Van Kan argues (42–43), and the records do support his contention. Joan's friend Dunois would not have doubted the divine origin of her voices, Raknem asserts, adding that it is also false for the Archbishop to "take a Shavian view of miracles and explain them in such a way that they lose their miraculousness" (191).

Again, one might say that these rationalistic touches in the play are far more noticeable when studying the work than when seeing it, for in Joan's presence we scarcely doubt her claim that the saints are real to her, and we never doubt the depth of her religious faith. It seems fair to conclude that although Shaw shaped her story for his own didactic ends, his rendering of her and her outlook is in the main true.

There is one important exception, however. In scene 6, when Joan amazedly learns, after her recantation, that she has avoided the stake only to be confined to prison, she seizes the recantation document and tears it to fragments, declaring that she dreads burning less than "the life of a rat in a hole" (145). Then in one of her longest speeches she says that she cannot live shut out from the light of the sky and the sight of the fields and the sound of the blessed church bells. If the choice be imprisonment or death, she emphatically chooses death.

But the real Joan was not nearly so emphatic. There is considerable ambiguity in the records as to whether she renounced her recantation because she felt she had betrayed her saints or because she herself had been betrayed by being placed in a particularly intolerable prison cell. When asked why she had resumed male attire after agreeing to give it up, she answered:

> "Because it is more lawful and suitable for me to resume it and to wear man's dress, being with men, than to have a woman's dress. I have resumed it because the promise made to me has not been kept; that is to say, that I should go to Mass and should receive my Saviour and that I should be taken out of irons."
> "Did you not abjure and promise not to resume this dress?"
> "I would rather die than be in irons! but if I am allowed to go to Mass, and am taken out of irons and put into a gracious prison, and [may have a woman for companion] [*sic*] I will be good, and do as the Church wills." (Murray, 136)

The promises to her had not been kept. And even worse, according to evidence given at the Rehabilitation, her woman's dress

> was taken away while she was asleep, and the English soldiers refused to give it back to her, offering in its stead the man's dress she had previously worn "which they emptied from a sack." She refused to wear it, reminding them that it was forbidden her; but at the last, at midday, finding them deaf to her remonstrance, she was obliged to rise and attire herself in the prohibited garments. The Dominican Brothers declared that she had been assaulted by an English milord, as she told them, and that she therefore con-

sidered it necessary to return to the protection of her old dress."
(Murray, 135n–36n)

It is evident that the English were furious with her recantation.
Even members of the court were bodily threatened by the outraged
soldiers. The English had not paid a huge ransom for her just to
keep her alive. They wanted her burned as a witch—for only thus
could they taint Charles's anointment at Rheims—and they made
her life in prison more grueling than ever. The prospect of an end-
lessly cruel imprisonment made Joan feel she had gained nothing
by her recantation.

Shaw read these passages but chose to ignore them, chose not
to have Joan in his play say that she would accept decent prison
conditions. Her only alternatives, as he presents them, are the
harsh prison or the stake. And the likely reason he narrowed the
choice was to have Joan illustrate and substantiate his contention
that capital punishment was preferable to long imprisonment, a
view he had argued for at great length, just one year before he began working on the play, in a prefatory essay to a volume on English prisons by his friends the Webbs, an essay he even refers to in
the preface to the play (34).

Apart from this noteworthy difference between the real and the
fictional Joan, Shaw is fairly faithful to her outlook. Can the same
be said, as well, of the historical significance that he ascribes to her
in the play? Is he right in scenes 4 and 6 in having ecclesiastical
and political figures think she embodies the spirit of Protestantism
and nationalism? Huizinga believes that Shaw is wrong. On the
subject of Protestantism, says the historian, "her spirit has nothing
in common with those of Huss and Wycliffe." She did not deliberately reject the Church, its teachings, or its rituals: "Protestantism
presupposes humanism, intellectual development, a modern spirit;
in her faith Joan of Arc was in the full sense of the word a primi-
tive" (237). The distinction is clear and up to a point appears entirely sound. But it curiously assumes that the intellectual precur-
sors of Protestantism, and its later founders, were entirely guided
by the light of reason and that some degree of personal assertiveness, dissatisfied feelings, and even national pride did not enter
into their opposition to Rome. Religion obviously involves emotional
as well as intellectual commitments, and Joan's insistence that

high officials of the Church were wrong to denigrate the divine origin of her voices seems precisely the kind of rejection of Catholic
authority that marked full-blown Protestantism decades later. Shaw
acknowledges in the preface that his Cauchon and Warwick are
more conscious and articulate about Joan's significance than their
real-life counterparts would have been, but essentially Shaw is
right that Joan represented a spirit of protest against the authority
of some high ecclesiastics, however particular and personal the occasion may have been, however much she may also have been devoted to religious rituals and considered herself an obedient child of
the Church. ("Protest" may be too strong a word and fit too neatly
for Shaw's purposes into "Protestantism," but Joan certainly dis-
agreed with the churchmen before her and, by keeping faith with
her voices, rejected the charge that her voices were diabolical.)

Shaw's contention that Joan heralded the Protestant threat to
the Church is supported by several of the statements we have
heard her make, such as "in case the Church should wish me to do
anything contrary to the command which has been given me of
God, I will not consent to it, whatever it may be" (Murray, 103); and
not the Church but "God must be served first" (Murray, 104). Several of the articles in the accusation against her, most notably article 62, further support Shaw's view:

> Jeanne hath laboured to scandalize the people, to induce them to
> believe in her talk, taking to herself the authority of God and His
> Angels, presumptuously seeking to seduce men from ecclesiasti-
> cal authority, as do the false prophets who establish sects of error
> and perdition and separate themselves from the unity of the
> Church; a thing pernicious in the Christian religion, which, if the
> Bishops did not provide against it, might destroy ecclesiastical
> authority; on all sides, in fact, raising up men and women who,
> pretending to have revelations from God and the Angels, will sow
> untruth and error—as hath already happened to many since this
> woman hath arisen and hath begun to scandalize Christian peo-
> ple and to publish her knaveries. (Murray, 363)

This woman was, to many churchmen, dangerous both in herself
and as an example to others. At the least, one imagines that
countless Europeans, unsympathetic to the English cause, must
have questioned the outcome of the Church's trial of Joan, and that

very questioning would have prepared the soil for the seeds of Protestant doctrines.

Shaw does not, of course, indicate that Joan herself was aware of her "Protestantism." (She not only thought of herself as a devoted child of the Church, but actually wrote a letter warning the Hussites that she would punish them if they did not return to the fold.) Yet he nevertheless highlights her "Protestantism" even beyond what the documents disclose. He omits her desire to submit her case to the Pope; and he gives her judgment an independence that she herself does not claim for it by changing her reply "I answer nothing from my own head; what I answer is by command of my Voices," to "What other judgment can I judge by but my own?" Shaw subtly makes Joan a heroine of his own Life Force religion, and in that religion there is no outside God sending messages or supplying instructions to the conscience; on the contrary, the only conscience and brain the Life Force possesses are supplied by human beings.

On the issue of nationalism, Shaw is more than half right though less original, since Shakespeare and Schiller (in his romantic tragedy *Die Jungfrau von Orléans*) had stressed Joan's nationalism. If she didn't create French patriotism, Joan certainly stimulated it, and all of her talk in the play about the injustice of English troops living in a country whose language was French is true to the real Joan's convictions. Repeatedly in her letters to the English king and his lords, Joan expressed the same sentiment as in her earliest one of 22 March 1428: "I am here sent by God, the King of Heaven, body for body, to drive you out of all France" (Murray, 37). But Shaw goes beyond this patriotic spirit to see in Joan an innovating advocate of the right of kings to control the nobility, and here he obviously claims too much. As Huizinga reminds us, national monarchies were from the beginning antithetical toward feudalism, and the conflict between the kings and the nobility had begun three centuries before Joan was born. "In England the monarchy had the upper hand in the conflict ever since the Conqueror. . . . In France the monarchy was triumphing over the lords slowly but surely" (238).

Joan's nationalism, however—and this aspect Shaw almost entirely omits—was by no means shared by all people living in the regions of France. The impression given by the play is that the invading English are conquering the embattled French, weakly led by the Dauphin until Joan's arrival on the scene. In reality, civil war prevailed, the Armagnac forces being led by Charles and the Burgundian faction by the Duke of Burgundy, who was allied with the English. Charles, by the Treaty of Troyes in 1420, had been disinherited by his mother, eliminated from the succession, and officially banished. The Burgundians and the English cemented their alliance by the marriage of Philip of Burgundy's sister Anne to the English Regent, the Duke of Bedford. Paris was controlled by the Burgundians and the English; the University of Paris, the great center of theological learning, was thoroughly hostile to the Dauphin Charles. Many people in the country loathed Charles, not least for his connivance in the assassination of John the Fearless of Burgundy in 1419. Those who wanted to establish a permanent accommodation with the English were the party of peace; Charles's was the war party. And, in the eyes of many people, Joan, by her bellicose actions, simply prolonged the war and the bloodshed. Shaw omits much of this not just for simplicity's sake, but to allow Joan to represent nationalism unqualifiedly, and also to free Cauchon, as we shall see in a moment, from political motives.

If, nevertheless, Shaw comes off moderately well in his prime claims about Joan's Protestantism and nationalism, is he equally accurate in his claim that the winds of medievalism waft through his play? Here, again, Shaw's success is not quite all that he claimed it to be, but it is nonetheless substantial even apart from the authenticity of Joan. Charles is more of a stage figure of fun than an actual prince, and he is made far more comic than true to the real nature of that serious, pious, and desperate man who later became king. Shaw has also been criticized for giving to Charles's court an unreal "atmosphere of noisy hilarity and noisy buffoonery" (Van Kan, 40). Furthermore, the spirit of farce hovering over the first two scenes seems more Shavian than medieval. Yet in every scene Shaw does include touches that convincingly situate the play in its period. We are reminded right from the outset of the hierarchical social structure, as Baudricourt assesses the exact social class of farmers that Joan's father represents and then talks of his own responsibility as the father's lord to see that Joan does not get into trouble. Throughout the play we are made aware of the feudal aristocracy's conflict with royalty and also of the pervasive power of the Catholic church. The characters discuss medieval fighting techniques and the practice of ransom; they enjoy looking at illuminated manuscripts; they make slighting remarks about Jews and Muslims. Pilgrimages to the Holy Land are mentioned, and we are shown several instances of the people's credulity, their appetite for miracles, and their total acceptance of witchcraft. Sometimes Shaw's ambition to have it both ways—to rub off the patina of time and promote a sense of familiarity but also to give the pastness of the past its due—renders the medieval touches too self-conscious and too pitched to an audience's later-day complacency, as when someone calls Pythagoras a fool for not believing in the earth's obvious flatness. But Shaw does give, if not the winds of medievalism, at least enough of its breezes to make us accept Joan's world as different from our own.

The great trial scene, however, does transport us back to another era and it rings true. We see the odd medieval courtroom procedures, learn that the prosecutor was called the promoter and that torture of heretics on trial was customary; we hear the strong rationale for the Inquisition and are told of the medieval attitude toward women's wearing of men's clothes; St. Athanasius is quoted, and the Executioner tells us some of his techniques. All the trappings of authenticity are visible, making Shaw seem more absent than in any other scene. Moreover, he here fulfills his desire of avoiding melodrama: the good Joan is not being dealt with by villains. Sincere and devout churchmen are striving to save her from excommunication and from being burned as a witch. Those who wish to torture her are rebuked by Cauchon, the chief judge. His fellow judge, Lemaître, the representative of the Inquisition, speaks as a patently kind and responsible man. From Joan's pathetic entrance—in chains, the pallor of imprisonment emphasized by her black clothing—to her exit in the grip of the soldiers taking her to the stake, the drama of this climactic scene seems so convincing that we never for a moment question its reality and its truth.

Yet it is precisely toward this compelling final scene that the most searching questions of historical authenticity have been put. No critic doubts the general surface truth of this scene. A quick glance at the actual proceedings seems to show a fair trial and a decent concern for the welfare of the accused, and Bishop Cauchon seems an unprejudiced judge. Yet a closer look at the documents reveals, as the eminent historian Pierre Champion has put it, that the trial was "a masterpiece of partiality under the appearance of the most regular of procedures," with Cauchon exhibiting "extreme skill in preventing this trial in the matters of faith from appearing to be visibly motivated by politics."[5] Or as a later historian, Victoria Sackville-West, has put it:

> Jeanne stood not the slightest chance from the first. Those who ask whether she was given a fair trial may here find their answer. She was given a trial conducted with all the impressive apparatus of ceremony, learning, and scholasticism that the Holy Catholic Church, the Court of the Inquisition and the University of Paris between them could command, but in essence the whole trial was a preordained and tragic farce.[6]

This conclusion would be assented to by Joan's first biographer in 1500 and by scores of later biographers; it was echoed by the Church itself in its later investigations of the trial, and it is a conclusion hard to avoid by anyone who scrutinizes the record.

Yet Shaw himself, strangely, avoided this conclusion, maintaining that the "judges were as straightforward as Joan herself" and that "they gave her a very long, a very careful, and a very conscientious trial. . . . They tried her quite mercifully" (Laurence, 6:221–22). Was Shaw somehow duped? Was his usually keen eye somehow blinded to the reality under the appearances? Or did he see the reality and choose for certain reasons to ignore it? This constitutes one of the most interesting issues raised by the play. And it is worth dwelling on even if it cannot be conclusively settled, for I think it takes us to the deeper springs in Shaw and thereby enables us to comprehend the hidden sources of the play's power.

There can be no questioning the fact that Shaw leaned over backwards to present Bishop Cauchon in a highly favorable light. Consider the following little exchange in the trial scene when Joan is accused of conversing with evil spirits:

> JOAN. Is the blessed St Catherine an evil spirit? Is St Margaret? Is Michael the Archangel?

COURCELLES. How do you know that the spirit which appears to
you is an archangel? Does he not appear to you as a naked
man?
JOAN. Do you think God cannot afford clothes for him?
The assessors cannot help smiling, especially as the joke is against
Courcelles.
LADVENU. Well answered, Joan. (6, 139)

Now this exchange is fairly accurately drawn from the actual trial
except that there Cauchon is the questioner and the joke is against
him! Shaw wanted to preserve one of the few touches of humor in
the trial records and a neat illustration of Joan's wit, but he did not
want to humiliate Cauchon or hint of any grounds for the Bishop to
be resentful towards the Maid.

Again, when Warwick in the last scene urges upon Cauchon
that Joan's death is a political necessity, and Cauchon indignantly
retorts that the Church is not subject to political necessity, we are
lead to believe him to be far more independent than he in fact was.
Though Shaw has him angrily insist in the fourth scene that he is
"no mere political bishop," the English had already rewarded Cauchon for past services not only with money but with membership in
their royal council. Only two weeks before Joan's capture, a letter
from England's King Henry VI reconfirmed Cauchon as counsellor,
at a fee of a thousand livres a year, with the words "in consideration of the good and loyal services the Reverend Father in God, Our
Beloved and Faithful Counsellor, the Bishop of Beauvais rendered
to my late and very dear Lord and Father . . . and renders to us at
the present time, in our councils and in other affairs and concerns"
(Rankin, 95). This bishop was put in charge of the trial out of his
own diocese, in the safe English-occupied city of Rouen, so that he
could ensure Joan's fate. He knew that finding Joan guilty would
well serve the political interests of his English friends and also the
political interests of his fellow clerics of the University of Paris, who
were dependent on the English for benefices. It is most unlikely
that he would say, as Shaw has him say at the end of the passage,
after Warwick leaves, "What scoundrels these English nobles are!"
(6, 126).

Yet again, when Joan realizes she will be burned and announces in despair that her voices have deceived her and she will
sign a confession of her sins, Ladvenu calls out elatedly, "Now God

be praised that He has saved you at the eleventh hour!" and Cauchon emphatically says "Amen!" (6, 142). But the trial records do
not at all show the Bishop saying this or giving any indication that
he is as sympathetic to the Maid's plight as Ladvenu. Nor, once
more, is there any indication in the records that Cauchon
protested, as he does in the play, that Joan at the close of the trial
is being precipitously handed over to the English soldiers.

These fabricated words enhance Cauchon's character in our
eyes, as do the words Shaw gives the Inquisitor to say: "Never has
there been a fairer examination within my experience, my lord. The
Maid needs no lawyers to take her part: she will be tried by her
most faithful friends, all ardently desirous to save her soul from
perdition" (6, 124). (Thus, incidentally, does Shaw take care of
Cauchon's failure to allow Joan to have any kind of defense counsel.) These are not the only words made up for the Inquisitor, Cauchon's alter ego. All the Inquisitor's words are of Shaw's creation.
Their effect throughout is to make it seem that a sage man, and a
representative of another arm of the Church, concurs entirely in
Cauchon's conduct of the trial and believes that Cauchon is, as he
says of him, wrestling the devil for her soul.

But Shaw not only touches up the portrait of Bishop Cauchon
with words added for him and about him. He also *omits* a good deal
that is far from attractive. Cauchon, for example, did not allow the
ascertained fact of Joan's virginity to be disclosed to the court,
preferring instead to let the trumped-up charge of promiscuity
stand against her. Cauchon also arranged to have one of the priests
ingratiate himself with Joan by pretending he came from her section of Lorraine, and this priest, Nicolas Loyseleur, became Joan's
confessor—and then reported what she told him to the Bishop for
use in interrogating and entrapping her. Moreover, Cauchon
blocked Joan's appeal to the Pope and the Council of Basle—
though saying after her death that she had refused to make such
an appeal. Cauchon also had his assistants promise her that her
irons would be removed and she would be allowed to attend mass if
she admitted her sins; but then he made sure that neither promise
was kept. The Bishop arranged that Joan's many interrogations
should be harassing, with questions thrown at her too fast for her
to answer. And—of considerable importance—though Joan was
being tried for sins against the Church, she was neither kept in an

ecclesiastical prison nor guarded by clerics or women as she requested and was her legal right, but instead was held in a lay prison watched over and sometimes abused by English soldiers.

Shaw does not dispute the fact that Cauchon, after her recantation, exclaimed to the English, "We shall get her yet"; nor his laughing, exulting cry to Warwick, after she withdrew her recantation and could not avoid being burned alive: "Farewell, farewell, it is done! Have good cheer!" Shaw knew that Cauchon had been driven from his see at Beauvais and then Rheims by Charles's troops, and that he had long been an enemy of the man Joan helped to crown at Rheims—Cauchon indeed had gained his bishopric for his political services in negotiating the treaty that eliminated Charles from the succession. Charles had now been anointed, but if Joan were proved a witch and a heretic, the coronation would be seriously tainted.[7] Shaw also knew that Cauchon had been in the pay of the English and actually served as go-between in arranging for Joan to be bought by them after her capture by John of Luxembourg. The distinguished lawyer Jean Lohier found the trial so ridden with illegalities and hatred that he told Cauchon it had absolutely no juridical value (Murray, xxi, xxii, 166–67). Nicolas de Houppeville, one of the few clerics who questioned the proceedings, was thrown into prison for his defiance of Cauchon (Murray, 190). Shaw knew all these things because the main book he consulted was T. Douglas Murray's translation of Jules Quicherat's multivolume *Process de Jeanne d'Arc* (published in the 1840s); in his introduction, Murray details some of Cauchon's biased behavior and rightly states that the Bishop was Joan's "declared and bitter enemy, and the mere instrument of her foes and gaolers" (xxii), and that he "sits in solitary infamy" (xx). And yet Shaw omitted all this information about Cauchon in order to portray him as a fair-minded judge!

Why was Shaw so false to the historical truth? His justification, in the preface, is twofold. Villains are out of place in a high tragedy, and the writer of Joan's tragedy must therefore "flatter Cauchon nearly as much as the melodramatist vilifies him." Moreover, the tragedy of Joan's murder is that it was not committed by murderers but by "normally innocent people in the energy of their righteousness," and if she had not been killed by such people, her death "would have had no more significance than the Tokyo earthquake, which burnt a great many maidens" (51).

Of course one could reply to Shaw's first point by noting that he is not writing high tragedy since the epilogue is in a comic vein, and also that high tragedies often *do* accommodate villains—Iago, Goneril, and Claudius are evil without the plays in which they appear being any the less high tragedies. Moreover, flattery is as false as vilification, and neither is appropriately used by a dramatist who claims to be presenting only the truth. Shaw's second point also seems at first sight equally fragile, for Joan's death carries grim significance even if (and especially if) its perpetrators were politically motivated priests.

It may well be that Shaw's emphasis on the harm that innocent but righteous people can do is far more important than historical accuracy. As A. M. Cohen astutely remarks,

> Always a great demolisher of complacency, [Shaw] alerts us to the fact that the persecution and murder of innocents may be done by 'normal' persons, perhaps a bit like ourselves. The historical instance may be wrong, because Cauchon and his associates were obvious knaves, but the moral is worth taking. In the aftermath of the World War, and his experience of so many ordinary people seized with jingoistic righteousness, this may have seemed the right comment on the tragedies of the epoch.[8]

Even so, it was not beyond Shaw's dramaturgic skills to have given Cauchon greater complexity, some mixture of motives, and to have allowed the audience to wonder about his sincerity and disinterestedness. Shaw does this wonderfully well with Major Barbara's father, Sir Andrew Undershaft, a man who merges the diabolical and the altruistic. A few hints of Cauchon as a man in conflict over Joan, his worldly and his Christian commitments pulling him in opposite directions, would not have weakened the last scene or made it melodramatic. The playwright need not have accepted the traditional blackening of Cauchon's character (though Cauchon obviously did most of the blackening himself), but to counter it by completely whitewashing him seems unnecessary—unless there are reasons undisclosed in the preface, and perhaps even unrecognized by the playwright. Such reasons we shall later attempt to fathom.

The Cauchon issue came up in Shaw's correspondence with Father Leonard several months before the play was begun. The Reverend demurred to the dramatist's description of the trial as "merciful and fair under the circumstances" and said it was illegal and unjust: "Cauchon was clearly out for her death." As an example take what he said, after her retraction, to the English, 'We shall get her yet.' " Shaw's lengthy reply to Leonard reveals fully both his understanding of the issue and his blind spots:

> I went into the subject with the usual impression of a corrupt tribunal, an infamously cruel Cauchon, an innocent victim, and a subsequent redress of a monstrous and tragic injustice. But I took care to avoid the histories, and read the process and nothing but the process; and immediately I saw that the usual impression is quite false. Of course I sympathized with the alleged redress and with the canonisation, and held the fraud of both to be pious fraud. None the less I want to insist on the fraud, because one of my missions in life is to make the Catholic Church conscious that it is more tolerant of private judgment than the Protestant persuasion, and to make the Protestant persuasion ashamed (if possible) of imagining that it grants a right of private judgment when it always attaches the condition that the private theologian must come to the same conclusion as the prayerbook.
>
> I called the first trial merciful, all things considered, because Joan was not put to the torture, though torture was almost a matter of course in such cases. There are of course two reasons that have nothing to do with mercy. One is that Joan kept affirming and reaffirming her heresy without any torture to wring confession from her. The other was the staggering effect on the inquisitors of her powerful common sense when they shewed her the instruments of torture, and threatened her with their application. "I daresay" said Joan, "if you torment me I shall say anything you want me to say to escape the pain; but the moment the pain is over I will take it all back." Still, the fact that she was not tortured, whatever the motive was, makes it impossible to maintain that her trial was a cruel one as trials went then.
>
> Cauchon's remark "We shall have her yet" was made when the English commander, who of course could not be got to understand anything except that he was determined to burn her, and was depending on the tribunal to hand her over to him, was so infuriated when her recantation led to the executioner being told that there was nothing doing, and he might go home, that he openly threatened the tribunal with violence. If Cauchon had not quieted him by some such assurance, he might have had his throat cut on the spot. Imagine yourself a good Catholic in the Holy Roman Empire phase, and a strong Unionist, and an old gentleman with ordinary prejudices as to female propriety. You

are confronted by a young woman under twenty, a rabid Sinn Feiner, who persists in wearing rational dress, or rather dressing like a common soldier, who has had the audacity to crown a king in a cathedral as if she were the Pope and he Charlemagne, who insists that she has had visits from apparitions who told her to do these things, and who—crowning heresy!—has said again and again that she does not believe the Church's teaching that these apparitions are devils sent to tempt her to sin, and that (like a good Protestant) she considers these messages from God to herself of higher authority than the Church. As a good Ulsterman might put it, she will suffer no priest to come between herself and her conscience; for she makes a conscience of what the Church assures her are hallucinations worked on her by the enemy of mankind. And to all reproof and exhortation she is contumacious as the devil himself.

Imagine, then, that when you actually fetch the executioner with his car and his faggots, her healthy objection to be burnt induces her to recant, without a pretence of change of heart, simply saying "I'll sign anything you want sooner than be burnt." Would you not have been infuriated by this evasion, and said to the English commander exactly what Cauchon said? And you would have been right, because when Joan heard that instead of being pardoned and released, she was to be imprisoned for life, she promptly said, "This is worse than burning: I never could stand being shut up." and took it all back, after which she was manifestly a relapsed heretic, and was burnt accordingly.

You now see my point. No informality in the constitution of the court or in the conduct of the English military people can alter the fact that if the court had been properly constituted the result must have been the same, even if Cauchon had been the kindest of men. The true statement of the case is not that there was an incorrect procedure at the first trial and a correct procedure at the revision and the canonisation, but that the first trial was uninspired and the canonisation inspired. . . . (*CL,* 3:798–99)

In the letter Shaw narrows Joan's choice to death or imprisonment rather than death or two different types of imprisonment—at the hands of the English or of the Church. One also notices the contemporary Irish context into which Shaw so readily translates the medieval French events, with Joan viewed as a rabid Sinn Feiner. But chiefly we see how Shaw enters the Bishop's mind with such penetrating sympathy that comprehension prompts pardon and the will to exonerate creates contradictions; in the third paragraph, for example, Cauchon is trying to quiet an "infuriated" English commander, but in the next paragraph it is Cauchon who is "infuriated" by Joan's evasion. Moreover, the old gentlemen Shaw describes, full of hostility to the young woman, should clearly not have served as her judge, though the dramatist himself does not reach that conclusion. Shaw defends the trial as merciful because torture was not used, but he does not now defend its fairness; Bishop Cauchon may not have been "infamously cruel," but by Shaw's own account he was scarcely open-minded. Shaw seems to accept Father Leonard's statement that "Cauchon was clearly out for her death," yet he refuses to recognize that this should have disqualified him from ruling even a medieval type of trial. He oddly overlooks the distinction between a judge and a prosecutor, though Cauchon both in the letter and in the play is a man who insists on Joan's guilt and will not allow her to disprove it.

The prejudiced Cauchon of this letter is not the whitewashed Cauchon of the play, but we can see here why Shaw felt that for his dramatic purposes he could clean up the Bishop. Historically, for Shaw, it did not matter what Cauchon's motives were: the outcome would have been the same "even if Cauchon had been the kindest of men." Joan was guilty of heresy and kept "affirming and reaffirming her heresy." The true conflict, he maintains—and arranges his play to illustrate it—is not between a cruel judge and an innocent victim but between opposing historical forces; the feudal nobility and the universal Church on one side, incipient nationalism and Protestantism on the other, the latter pair embodied in Joan. To attend to the petty detail of a prejudiced judge is, for Shaw, to blur the remorseless processes of history that the play is unfolding for our enlightenment.

This is undoubtedly Shaw's most powerful argument, and he enunciated it on several occasions, even as late as 1948, declaring: "For all I know or care the worst that Clemens and Lang wrote about them [Cauchon and Lemaître] may have been deserved. The real parties in the case were the Catholic Church, the Holy Office, and militant Whig Feudalism" (Laurence, 243). This argument undergirds the play's most vital issue of change versus order. But it is not historically accurate. Joan's "Protestantism" cannot finally be separated from her "nationalism." Her religious "heresy" is entangled with her politics—both for her and for Cauchon. Shaw's letter makes clear the intermixing of the two for Cauchon but he omits this in the play. He also omits it for Joan. Yet had Joan crowned a king whom Cauchon *supported*, and been told to do so by saintly voices, Cauchon would never have questioned either her loyalty to the Church or the authenticity of the voices. Shaw wants to make Joan representative of early Protestantism, and in a sense she was, but her protests were prompted solely by certain churchmen finding her voices diabolical because she favored Charles VII. Her Protestantism was not, as Shaw would have it, an independent response to the Church as such. It was a consequence of her political mission.

Joan fully understood this. She complained from the beginning over the composition of the court, asking that some clerics from her own party should be included in the sixty odd assessors who were present and paid by the English. She knew Cauchon was a political enemy, an ally of the English, and that the men he and the pro-English University of Paris appointed to the court were also hostile to King Charles. She knew that the other clergymen who had investigated her the preceding year at Charles's behest, at Poitiers, had found nothing diabolical in her voices and apparitions; on the contrary, they accepted the possibly divine source and believed that her later successes validated her claims. The priests who accompanied her army and escorted her as she marched victoriously into Orléans did not believe she was a sorceress or a heretic. Having had the Archbishop of Rheims—the metropolitan of Cauchon's see—and other high churchmen on Charles's side regard her favorably, Joan knew (what Shaw curiously disregards) that the Church was not uniformly against her and that therefore Cauchon could not be speaking for the entire Church but only for that section of it which backed the English and benefited from English patronage.[9] Joan knew, in short, that the particular churchmen now conducting the trial were enemies deploying charges of irreligious behavior as a political weapon. ("Political passions and interests, above all else, divided the judges and the accused," as Pierre Champion states it [509].) Joan tried to appeal over their heads to the Pope, but Cauchon blocked her request and punished any clerics who advised her to make such an appeal. Joan accused Cauchon, not the Church, of sentencing her to the stake and said bitterly to him on her last day, "Bishop, I die through you!" (Murray, 158).[10]

Shaw disregards all this because he is using Joan and Cauchon to build, as it were, a Hegelian, capitalized theory of History. For him, history looms over the events, and human beings are subordinate to huge and inexorable historical movements. As a Marxist, he sees Joan as an agent of civilization's unilinear progress, nationalism and Protestantism being necessary steps on the long road to capitalism and then socialism. Individuals, even the worthiest, must sacrifice themselves or be sacrificed to promote that forward movement. For Shaw it distorts our understanding of the historical process to focus on the behavior of a single priest called Peter Cauchon. With or without a Cauchon, the Church was historically doomed to lose some of its power to emergent Protestantism. And since this was so, it was necessary for the Church to try to postpone its fate by ridding itself of dangerous proto-Protestants like Joan. It had no choice. Joan's fate was historically determined, her execution inevitable.

Such was more or less Shaw's interpretation of Joan's trial, and the burden of much of his argument in the preface. Small truths could be sacrificed to what he regarded as the essential truth. For him, that truth shines forth more vividly if he shows the Church as unified and uniformly convinced of Joan's guilt, and shows its action as purely theological rather than political—a reasoned, albeit impassioned, opposition to the Protestant principle incarnate in Joan. Hence, for Shaw, her words alone, not the political partisanship or the vested ecclesiastical interests of her accusers, brought on her death.

Shaw felt that placing Joan in this larger framework of history increased her significance. Yet it can in fact diminish her. As Huizinga expresses it:

> Joan of Arc as the subject of a historical hypothesis, as Shaw would have it, an exponent of certain ways of thinking—there is something annoying in it. In her irreducible uniqueness she can be understood only by means of a sense of sympathetic admiration. She does not lend herself to being used to clarify currents and concepts of her day. Her own personality attracts all the attention as soon as one touches on her history. She is one of the few figures in history who cannot be anything but protagonists, who are never subordinate, always an end and never a means. (238–39)

Huizinga's criticism applies more to the preface than the play, which, with the exception of the tent scene and perhaps the epilogue, does show Joan as a protagonist whose personality attracts all our attention and sympathetic admiration. There is indeed an enriching double perspective between Joan seen as an admirably willful independent creature and, contrastingly, as an agent of European history. Nevertheless, the trial scene, for all its power, does bend the actual events to fit a historical hypothesis, and to that extent it falsifies Joan's story.

Would that story have been different with a judge other than Cauchon? Shaw obviously preferred to think not, but we cannot be certain. The vice-Inquisitor, Jean Lemaître, was by all accounts a reluctant participant at the trial. Had he been fully in charge and not subservient to the dominating personality of Cauchon, or had a judge less beholden to the English interests been in charge, the result might have been somewhat different. From the beginning of the trial, Joan might have been allowed to stay in a Church prison, attended by women; she might have been provided with counsel and allowed to have people speak on her behalf; her appeal to the Pope and the Council of Basle might have been permitted; and at the last a sentence of imprisonment in a Church prison might have been arranged. Her death was not inevitable.

Of course, it can be argued that whatever may be said of Shaw as a historian, as a dramatist he benefits by having simplified and omitted and distorted certain historical facts. The issues are more neatly and schematically presented, as in the tent scene, when nationalism is made Warwick's sole concern and Protestantism Cauchon's, and the two men are shown as mutually suspicious rather than cordially allied (as they were); or in the next scene, when the Archbishop of Rheims denounces Joan's voices (118) and thereby implies that the Church is uniformly against her (which it was not); or in the trial scene, when heresy is the dominant issue and the churchmen seem uninvolved in political matters (though they were). But this argument belittles Shaw's ingenuity as a dramatist. As suggested earlier, it would have required only a few changes to make Cauchon a more ambiguous figure, one perhaps using theological principles to mask resentment and political ambition. In other words, Shaw is not at all sacrificing truth to write a more effective play but, rather, to promote a view of man and of history that he now urgently wants to believe and disseminate. He wants to believe that Joan and the Church were irreconcilable agents of historical forces, Joan being the means by which history sped its unfolding. To some extent he wants to depersonalize history, and this despite the fact that Joan is obviously a heroic person. Finally, he urgently wants to avoid dealing with the relationship of human evil to history.

What accounts for the urgency? What made Shaw so reluctant to impugn the purity of Cauchon's motives? The answer carries us to our final chapter and to the most interesting drama of the playwright's later years, as well as to a prime reason for his deep engagement with Joan's story. But as we take our departure from considering Shaw as historian, it is well to remember that despite the strange whitewashing of Bishop Cauchon, *Saint Joan* does possess a great deal of historical truth, not so much as Shaw claimed but more in fact than any other play written about her up to that time. This is an even more remarkable accomplishment when we remember that Shaw was a didactic writer who usually left a strong personality imprint on his work. In this play he restrains himself admirably and subordinates himself to depicting Joan's character and career. It is to his credit that *Saint Joan* (apart from the epilogue) is his least recognizably "Shavian" work and also has far more veracity than any of his nine other history plays.

10

The Inner Conflict

I must lie down where all the ladders start,
In the foul rag-and-bone shop of the heart.
—William Butler Yeats[1]

We have noticed earlier a central difference between the play and
its epilogue, the former exonerating Cauchon and his fellow
churchmen, the latter faulting them for blindly following the law.
This same contradiction appears in the preface as well though it is
masked by the forcefulness of Shaw's prose. He criticizes the
Church for not reconciling itself to modern science, for not tolerating heresy, and even for not inculcating and encouraging free
thought. (He omits mention of how such radical changes would be
compatible with Catholic doctrines.) He also insists, as in the play,
that Joan was in spirit a Protestant, and he backhandedly compli-
ments the Church by saying that "her canonization was a magnificently Catholic gesture as the canonization of a Protestant saint by
the Church of Rome" (37).

In the unrevised draft of the preface, Shaw went even further
in attacking the Church. He finds its present position on Joan's
voices absurd and advises it to "cease to nurture Joan's private revelations as supernatural revelations." He wants the Church to get
rid of its "superstitious rubbish," and its "belief in legends," and he
claims that every Protestant cherishes "all the Catholic dogmas in
one form or another." (This last phrase suggests how cavalierly he
regarded the Church's dogmas.) Though not a believer in God, he
nevertheless proclaims that "the law of God is the law of change,

and whenever any Church sets itself against change as such, it is setting itself against the law of God" (Tyson, 104).

Yet for all its general strictures on the Catholic Church, the preface finally comes down in favor of the Church's original actions against Joan. She flatly refused, Shaw says, to accept the Church's interpretation of God's will and to abandon her own; and she "made it clear that her notion of a Catholic Church was one in which the Pope was Pope Joan." How then, Shaw asks, "could the Church tolerate that?" How could it defer to a girl who "was always ready with a private revelation from God to settle every question and fit every occasion?" In short, "the Church could not tolerate her pretensions without either waiving its authority or giving her a place beside the Trinity during her lifetime and in her teens, which was unthinkable. Thus an irresistible force met an immovable obstacle, and developed the heat that consumed poor Joan." In these assertions Shaw is but echoing the arguments of Bishop Cauchon. And he concludes by announcing that "for us the first trial stands valid" (30–32).

Is there anything else, then, that the Church might have done after rightly convicting her of heresy? Yes, Shaw provisionally answers—it could simply have excommunicated her. But when he finally examines that possibility, after a few digressive pages, he decides it would have been impractical. An independent person like Joan might have founded a Church of her own—the spirit of Protestantism was in the air—and she might have affirmed her church "to be the temple of the true and original faith from which her persecutors had strayed. But as such a proceeding was, in the eyes of both Church and State at that time, a spreading of damnation and anarchy, its toleration involved a greater strain on faith in freedom than political and ecclesiastical human nature could bear" (40). The Church had to act, since tolerance has its limits in all societies. "We may prate of toleration as we will," Shaw concludes, "but society must always draw a line somewhere between allowable conduct and insanity or crime, in spite of the risk of mistaking sages for lunatics and saviors for blasphemers. We must persecute, even to the death" (41). Thus Shaw in the end echoes the words of his Inquisitor as well as Cauchon.

It is impossible to reconcile the support that Shaw the preface writer here gives to the Church with the support Shaw the dramatist gives to Joan's resounding final plea: "O God that madest this beautiful earth, when will it be ready to receive Thy saints? How long, O Lord, how long?" Apparently when one descends from the stage to the world, those self-appointed saviors who are "always ready with a private revelation from God to settle every question" cannot and should not be tolerated. Joan's ringing words offer no help in drawing the line "between allowable conduct and insanity or crime." (In 1898, in his notes to *Caesar and Cleopatra*, Shaw himself had called Joan a half-witted genius, "enjoying the worship accorded by all races to certain forms of insanity" [*CW*, 9:210]). For answers to the difficult issues presented by his play, Shaw seems as much at a loss as the rest of us.

The preface offers no solution to the problem of what should have been done with Joan. (As we saw earlier, Shaw could not accept the solution of imprisoning her, since he felt that imprisonment was worse than death. And he erroneously maintains in the preface, as in the play, that Joan deliberately chose death "as an alternative to life without liberty" [21], omitting the alternative she proposed of life in a church prison, tended by women—which would also have offered the possibility of eventual ransom or rescue or escape.) Shaw abhors her being burned at the stake, but he is silent about what should have been done with her. Perhaps he would have favored, as he later did for enemies of the state, simply a painless technique of execution; for him the cruelty was not in the killing of social undesirables but only in the method.[2]

There is, of course, no reason Shaw should be held accountable for not supplying a solution or telling us how society should deal with its most threatening heretics. The value of the preface lies precisely in indicating that Shaw was deeply troubled by this question and was of two minds about its solution. The preface's uncertainties prove that it was not merely forensic skill or a sympathetic imagination that allowed the playwright to give eloquence to the words of Cauchon and the Inquisitor. He himself partly shared their feelings and views. The power of the play thus derives in part from a deep-seated conflict in Shaw himself, and the tragic dilemmas of the play reflect tragic dilemmas in his own mind.

Further evidence of Shaw's preoccupation with these dilemmas is provided by an essay he wrote in October of 1922, less than two months before his first letter to Father Leonard about Joan. The essay, published posthumously, was entitled "On Ritual, Religion, and the Intolerableness of Tolerance."[3] (A second typescript bore the alternative title "The Church versus Religion.") Phrases here and there remind one of the play soon to come, as when, like his Archbishop of Rheims talking skeptically about "miracles" fabricated to augment belief, Shaw speaks of the Catholic Church providing "sham miracles" to save the souls of simple peasants (160). Or when he boasts of his Protestant spirit and says that there should be no priestly intervention "between me and my God" and no visible image is needed for him "to apprehend as much of my relation to the universe as is humanly apprehensible" (164), he anticipates Cauchon's praise of Joan in the epilogue for having raised the eyes of the peasant girls till "they see that there is nothing between them and heaven." And when he insists that in spiritual matters "I must interpret what I see for myself" (164), he is anticipating the courtroom line he gives to Joan—which, we have seen, she never said—"What other judgment can I judge by but my own."

But it is in the essay's pervasive concern with toleration, and a double-mindedness about it, that we see its common ground with *Saint Joan* and the preface. Eventually in the essay Shaw comes out on the side of religious tolerance—"we had better be careful how we judge one another" (170), but not before he has announced with approval that "Christ was not tolerant" (158), that "toleration as an expediency may be very advisable, but as a principle it is out of the question" (157–58), and that "no man will tolerate what he believes to be a false and mischievous religion whilst he has the means of persecuting and suppressing it." Lenin is mentioned and put into conjunction with George Washington; and although Lenin's persecutions are not mentioned, possible grounds for defending them are established by such remarks as "I do not believe there is a man or woman on earth who cannot be fitted with a case in which he or she is an uncompromising advocate of ruthless persecution" (157). Shaw admires those who are willing to sacrifice heroically for their convictions; he is faintly contemptuous of the tolerant "Laodicean man of the world" (153) who makes up "the easy-going majority" (156). He almost reluctantly concludes that "the moral of all this is that you must suffer your neighbour to serve God in his own way" (167). The very inconclusiveness of the essay may be the reason Shaw did not arrange for its publication.

The dilemma over tolerating heresy, it is important to recognize, would not have been so acute a dozen years earlier. Throughout his early years Shaw was a political rebel. Except for a few years as vestryman and councillor for the London borough of St. Pancras, he was an outsider, peppering those in power with tracts and essays and plays. As a socialist, he was against all the capitalist powers of his day. Opposition, heresy, unorthodoxy, defiance— these were congenial stances, and he would rush to the defense of his fellow radicals or of those who, like Roger Casement or the Fenians, disregarded the authority of the British government. Joan obviously appealed to Shaw because he saw in her some of his own traits, and to a certain extent he emphasized those traits in depicting her personality. Like her, he followed his own inner light, felt he was a servant of the Life Force (which he asserts she called God), and enjoyed bossing people around. He, too, had been an outsider—brash, humorous, energetic, and combative. As he insists she was never for a moment "a romantic young lady," but rather someone who would have nothing to do with sex, so, too, he prided himself on being unromantic and in his maturity transcending sexual desire. An ascetic in cuisine, Shaw notes that Joan was one also. An intellectual, he calls Joan one, too. He ascribes to her the same overweening self-confidence that he was often accused of possessing. Like Joan, Shaw also knew what it was to feel isolated and rejected: his highly unpopular opinions on World War I resulted in fierce attacks on him and social ostracism, including being forced to resign from the Dramatists' Club, of which he was the most eminent member. He thought himself a farseeing genius and credited Joan with being one. And when he says of Joan's voices, "there are people in the world whose imagination is so vivid that when they have an idea it comes to them as an audible voice, sometimes uttered by a visible figure" (P, 11), he is equally describing his own inspirations as a dramatist.

A dozen years earlier, this Shavian personality of Joan would have been used by the playwright, I believe, to expose the pretensions and devices of ecclesiastical and secular authority. (At the close of *Androcles and the Lion*, written twelve years earlier, Shaw began his commentary by saying: "In this play I have presented one of the Roman persecutions of the early Christians, not as the conflict of a false theology with a true, but as what all such persecutions essentially are: an attempt to suppress a propaganda that seemed to threaten the interests involved in the established law and order, *organized and maintained in the name of religion and justice by politicians who are pure opportunist Have-and-Holders*" [*CW*, 14:147; emphasis added].) A dozen years earlier, Cauchon would have been shown to be what he was—an opportunistic political bishop, a willing servant of English interests, pretending to be fair-minded and merciful. But in 1917 a government appeared in Russia whose authority Shaw fully supported and against whom any rebelliousness was to be condemned. Shaw openly declared himself to be a communist and was an enthusiastic supporter of the Soviet Union from its inception. In 1921 he sent Lenin a copy of his new play *Back to Methuselah*, with the handsome dedication: "to Nicolas Lenin—the only European ruler who is displaying the ability, character and knowledge proper to his responsible position—from Bernard Shaw" (*CL*, 4:103). (It was an inscription the Kremlin proudly printed and widely circulated.) Lenin was vigorously criticized not only in the capitalist press in the West but also by many Marxists, such as H. M. Hyndman, and by many Fabian socialists, for his ruthless stamping out of all opposition—and the numbers of those he had executed soon mounted into the thousands. Lenin was accused of barbarous cruelty. (After the socialist Bertrand Russell met Lenin, he commented on the Mongolian cruelty in his eyes and his laughter.) Lenin's supporters scoffed at these charges and the denigration of their hero, and among Lenin's—and later Stalin's—most vocal supporters was Shaw. For him, those heretics who defied the authority of the Soviet government were undermining the revolution. The big train of history was now moving fast, and mere individuals had better get out of the way. Commissar Felix Djerzinsky, who was to become chief of the NKVD (later the KGB), went around the country like a one-man inquisitor summarily shooting people who did not obey government orders, and Shaw so admired this man—"gentle Djerzinsky" as he called him (*Prefaces*, 639)—that he kept a photograph of him on his mantelpiece.

Suddenly, in the soul of George Bernard Shaw there were two people—on the one side the old rebel and individualist, the champion of private judgment, and on the other the new defender of law and order, of the duty of dictatorial governments to exterminate all dissidents. And these are the two people vying in Shaw as he writes his play about a heretic who defies the powers that be. If Shaw obviously identifies with Joan, he also, though less obviously, identifies with Cauchon. And for him to face the evil in Cauchon might have required him to face the possible evil in the Djerzinskys and Lenins and Stalins of the world. Shaw temperamentally and philosophically had difficulty accepting evil. This perhaps helped to make him a great writer of comedy. But it also made him avert his eyes from darker impulses that could lurk behind the actions of communist leaders and behind their self-justifying invocations of history.

To make theater audiences see the past as a clash of large, almost impersonal forces would enable them to see the present in the same way, undisturbed by the mere personal pains of ordinary individuals. Protestantism (as *Saint Joan* would seek to demonstrate) had begun to shove aside Catholicism just as Socialism was now shoving aside Capitalism, and the mere human victims—heroic or weak as the case might be—had to accept being hurt. Thus Shaw could write to a Russian friend in 1920, "As to compulsory labor, I have been declaring for years past that Socialism without compulsory labor and ruthless penalization of idleness and exploitation is nothing but a hopeless confusion of Socialism with Liberalism" (*CL,* 3:702–3). To justify Joan's trial and Catholicism's treatment of heretics was by implication to justify Communism's treatment of *its* heretics.

Eric Bentley has written that Joan's trial "was as shameless and corrupt a frame-up as anything in Soviet annals."[4] But for Shaw—who defended the Soviet purges—this would be a narrow view of both Joan's and Soviet trials, a failure to see them from the cleansing alpine perspective of history. Ruthlessness is the forceps as history gives birth to great new movements. But the agents of history take no joy in ruthlessness. That is why Shaw's invocations of history in his play—nationalism, Protestantism—are so urgently important to him. Justifying historical necessity in the fifteenth century becomes a way of sanctioning historical necessity in his own time. As Joan's fate was "inevitable," so, too, was the fate of those in Russia who opposed the new imperatives of history. And the authority figures, Cauchon and the Inquisitor, must be shown as ruthfully doing their historically imposed tasks. No mere fallible men, they are, like Lenin and Djerzinsky, servants of vast historical forces, as is Joan herself.

(Shaw could not avert his eyes entirely from the joy some men could take in ruthlessness. He knew too much about life and himself to pretend that evil did not exist. But he seemed determined to keep that knowledge on the fringes of his belief in great men. Not all the churchmen in the trial scene are as benign as Cauchon and the Inquisitor. D'Estivet, the prosecutor, is said to be "vulpine beneath his veneer"; Courcelles is accused of wanting to torture Joan for the mere pleasure of it; and Chaplain Stogumber craves to see her burned. Yet the paramount authority figures—the Bishop and the Inquisitor, and even Warwick—are kept free of any taint of sadism.)

One might schematically say, then, that Joan represents the earlier, rebellious, and high-spirited Shaw, and Cauchon the later, grimmer, and authority-supporting Shaw. The conflict between Joan and Cauchon, then, is in some sense a conflict between the younger and the older dramatist. In the play the older Shaw wins, but in the high-spirited epilogue the younger Shaw returns to triumph. In the preface, Shaw's two selves are in contention, with one self insisting on the need to "persecute, even to the death," on the need to counter the "lies about Lenin," and the other self insisting on the importance of individual freedom. But, ominously, if a choice must be made between society and the individual's right to speak out, society must prevail, for "the degree of tolerance attainable at any moment depends on the strain under which society is maintaining its cohesion" (41). Words like these are invariably used by dictators, Lenin among them, to smash all opposition.

Much of the confusion in the preface comes from the two Shaws stumbling over each other. Admittedly, as we have seen in chapter 7, it is a difficult issue. But Shaw up to 1917 would have argued far more forcefully for individuality. Although he would have granted (as all but anarchists must grant) that society must finally maintain its cohesion against an individual whose actions threaten it, he would have warned that "the interests involved in the established law and order" (as he phrased it) are apt to be too quick to suspend the rights of the individual, equating their own interests with society's. Shaw fully recognized this truth as it applied to capitalist society, but he ignored it when thinking of communist society. Up to 1917, again, Shaw would never have had a good word for the Inquisition. In the 1911 preface to *The Doctor's Dilemma*, for example, he terms the Inquisition an abomination (*CW*, 78); a year earlier, in the *Misalliance* preface, he condemns "the ruthlessness of Grand Inquisitors" (*CW*, 66); as late as 1915, in the preface to *Androcles and the Lion*, he speaks of "the cruel fanaticism of inquisitors" (*CW*, 45). Yet in the political *Prefaces* he would write after *Saint Joan*, he reverses his stance on the Inquisition; and though he somewhat worries over toleration, he ever more emphatically defends the autocratic state and the summary execution of those who defy its authority. Here, for instance, is how the 1933 preface to the play *On the Rocks* begins, under the subheading "Extermination":

> In this play a reference is made by a Chief of Police to the political necessity for killing people: a necessity so distressing to the statesmen and so terrifying to the common citizen that nobody except myself (as far as I know) has ventured to examine it directly on its own merits, although every Government is obliged to practise it on a scale varying from the execution of a single murderer to the slaughter of millions of quite innocent persons. . . . We must strip off the whitewash and find out what is really beneath it. Extermination must be put on a scientific basis if it is ever to be carried out humanely and apologetically as well as thoroughly.... if we desire a certain type of civilization and culture we must exterminate the sort of people who do not fit into it. (*Prefaces*, 353)

And he proceeds not only to defend what he terms the Russians' "Inquisition," and the "overwhelming necessity for exterminating the peasants, who still exist in formidable numbers" (363), but also to hope that even when the communists eliminate all private property and everyone has an equal share in the national wealth, the practice of extermination will not be discontinued but rather continued "much more openly and intelligently and scientifically than at present" (357). The debate later in this preface between Jesus and Pilate is a replay in another key of the confrontation between Joan and the churchmen—between the younger and the older Shaw—and again, after all is said, our dramatist still ends up defending the government's use of terror and extermination.

To what end? Ostensibly, to build a utopia. But not on the old Fabian assumption that the obstacle to utopia lay in the economic system, for now Shaw tells us that "the notion that a civilized State can be made out of any sort of human material is one of our old Radical delusions. As to building Communism with such trash as the Capitalist system produces it is out of the question" (363).

What is to be done with the trash? In the following year, 1934, he tells us, at first by a dramatic fable entitled *The Simpleton of the Unexpected Isles*—in which millions of people are vaporized—and then by statements in the preface. There Shaw insists that the real-life moral of his dramatic fable is the need to set up public tribunals to investigate all citizens of the country and make sure they are paying their way in society: "We need no Bolshevik propaganda to lead us to this obvious conclusion; but it makes the special inquisitionary work of the Tcheka intelligible. For the Tcheka was simply carrying out the executive work of a constitution which had abolished the lady and gentleman exactly as the Inquisition carried out the executive work of a catholic constitution which had abolished Jupiter and Diana and Venus and Apollo" (641). Rather than finding inquisitions deplorable, the author of *Saint Joan* heaps praise on them. "There should always be an Inquisition available to consider whether these human nuisances should not be put out of their pain, or out of their joy as the case may be" (643). He claims in another preface that the Soviet secret police is an updated version of the Inquisition—"essentially the system is that of the old Christian Catholic church"—and he applauds it (348).

After making a trip in 1931 to Russia, Shaw writes admiringly of the Soviet government "for frankly shooting anarchists and syndicalists,"[5] and for shooting members of the high bourgeoisie —though he complains that "it is not done quite as thoroughly as one could desire" (Geduld, 82). He ponders the following question: "How is it then that the leaders of the Russian revolution have been able to do what I cannot do: that is, set up an effective inquisition to enforce to the death the dogma that forsytism—parasitism—is the sin against the Holy Ghost, and that though all other sins may be forgiven, to it there is only one reaction: bang!?" (Geduld, 94).

As late as 1944, after five years of war against Hitler, when the monstrous crimes of the Gestapo and the concentration camps were well known, Shaw could still declare that "we shall have to revive the Inquisition. We need that institution very badly"; and he could not "conceive of a stable civilization without a constantly functioning inquisition."[6]

These words of praise for the inquisitional principle, and its modern embodiment in the Soviet Union, help us to understand why Shaw was so strangely sympathetic to Cauchon and the Inquisitor in *Saint Joan*, and why the play offers a positive depiction of the Inquisition. As remarked a few pages back, when Shaw was justifying Joan's trial and Catholicism's treatment of heretics, he was by implication justifying communism's treatment of *its* heretics.

Since modern heretics must be killed, the means of spreading heresy must be destroyed also; and Shaw comes not only to praise the Catholic Church for its undemocratic methods of governing—Stalin is admired for being like a Pope—but also to denounce "individual liberty," "freedom of speech and Press," and "constitutional safeguards against tyranny." All these, he asserts, "are now played out. They never stood disinterested examination as arguments" (Geduld, 85). One wonders whether Shaw at all remembered his own powerful arguments on behalf of free speech in the prefaces to *Mrs. Warren's Profession* and *The Shewing-Up of Blanco Posnet*?

Occasionally in these antidemocratic, proliquidation writings Shaw recognizes what his earlier self knew, as when he says that there is a need for "freedom of thought and facility of change to keep pace with thought" (*Prefaces*, 350). He also knows that in the inquisitional Soviet Union a young Bernard Shaw—jobless, spending his time writing unpublished novels, living largely on his mother's income—would never survive the public tribunals. Yet, though he is at times worried about the intolerance of the Soviet system, he seems obsessed with justifying governmental inquisitions. (I have elsewhere tried to account for this obsession.[7]) He also employs words that seek to neutralize the horror of his proposals: he speaks of "humanely and judiciously" liquidating people, of using "serious and responsible" tribunals, of doing it all "scientifically." He carefully states his opposition to torture and advocates quick methods of killing. Yet beneath these embellishments, all but the most bemused Shaw idolaters can hear a sadistic note.[8] Shaw's claim that the cruelty lies solely in the method of extermination and not in the taking of a life reveals a critical blind spot in his thought, and it accounts for his failure to notice the sadism in many of his latter-day essays. He was far more sensitive to the presence of this sadistic impulse in earlier years, and in fact the very structure of several of his plays, including *Saint Joan*, is designed to accommodate and then defeat the sadism.

Although this is a distasteful biographical matter, we must consider it briefly, since it bears not only upon Shaw's later political support for totalitarian regimes, both of the left and the right, but more especially upon our play and its epilogue. We may approach this point with an observation made by one of Shaw's best biographers, St. John Ervine. At the moment when Joan in the last scene finishes her freedom speech, "that is the moment when the rage of the sadistic celibate priests bursts into horrible fury, and the Maid is declared to be a relapsed heretic and sent to the market place to be burnt alive" (499). That is the moment the Inquisitor in the play declares her to be "infected with the leprosy of heresy," and Cauchon declares her to be "a member of Satan" to be cast out and abandoned. A later critic, Maurice Valency, expands upon the element of sadism in the scene. The part of Joan, he says, presents a problem even though Shaw tried to make her mannish: "The danger of having such a character played by a handsome actress with a good figure does not seem to have troubled Shaw." Yet "it would be naive to expect to expect that a beautiful woman, becomingly dressed in tight-fitting clothes, would deliberately obscure her femininity on the stage. Consequently, Joan's trial takes place in a perversely erotic atmosphere which no amount of serious discussion can dispel. Regardless of the author's intention, it is virtually impossible to disguise the sadistic nature of the proceedings" (383–84).

Now as we recall, this perversely erotic, sadistic atmosphere is also present to a lesser degree at the end of the preceding scene, when the men join in baiting Joan and making her miserable. And, significantly, this hurting of a young woman is not a unique phenomenon in Shaw's canon. We may remember the dreadful moment when Major Barbara's faith in the Salvation Army is destroyed and she is on the verge of tears, or the equally dreadful moment in act 4 of *Pygmalion* when Eliza Doolittle is so cruelly ignored by Professor Higgins after winning his bet for him that she wishes she were dead. After creating these sadistic climaxes, Shaw—as if in guilt and for masochistic fulfillment—turns his plays around to allow the women to triumph, Eliza actually forcing Higgins to moan "You have wounded me to the heart." Of course Joan's dreadful death did not permit her to "get her own back" as Eliza and Barbara do. It may be that Shaw, for all of the conscious reasons prompting him to write an epilogue, was also subconsciously impelled to repeat a pattern established in some of the other plays wherein the heroine is first tormented and then triumphs.

In the epilogue, Joan certainly gets her own back against all of the men who have hurt her. And if the tone of the epilogue is often strained in its efforts at humor, it is perhaps because Shaw is seeking to atone for the obscure and guilty pleasure he took in her earlier abasement and agony; he is seeking to say, as it were, that this is only a play, a mere playing with fire, and any sadistic satisfaction he or we enjoyed was only make-believe. The structure of the entire work, in short, expresses the same impulse that led Shaw to create in Stogumber a quasisadist who is finally filled with remorse.

It is no disparagement of Bernard Shaw to recognize this sadistic strand in his work or his character, or even to say that he may have been attracted to Joan's story in part because of its intrinsic cruelty. We may like our playwrights to be saints, but saints may be able to write only mediocre drama. The question is not whether sadism and masochism are in Shaw's work—anyone who reads the one-act play *The Music Cure* will see how Shaw himself joked about this fact—the question is what the dramatist was able to create out of the foul rag-and-bone shop of his heart. And it was out of his sadism, and his powerful resistance to it, that Shaw derived some of his creative energy and his material.

Seen from this biographical perspective, on the inner stage of Shaw's psyche, John de Stogumber—apart from that English jingoism which Shaw satirizes—is a self-admonitory figure. He is full of destructive impulses uncurbed by reason or imagination. Shaw himself was not without those impulses, but he knew he also had a powerful intellect and imagination, and therefore an obligation to imagine reality. "It is so easy to talk when you don't know," Stogumber moans. "You madden yourself with words; you damn yourself because it feels good to throw oil on the flaming hell of your own temper. But when it is brought home to you; when you see the thing you have done; when it is blinding your eyes, stifling your nostrils, tearing your heart, then—then—" (6, 149). It is imagination's role to see the act before it is irredeemably done, and Stogumber is in one sense Shaw's warning to himself, an acting out, of the perils of drugging oneself with words, even perhaps the words *history* and *revolution* and *capitalism* and *proletariat* and *bourgeoisie* and that modern equivalent of The Church known as The Party.

The play itself can also be regarded as self-admonitory, at least insofar as Joan in her suffering brings home to Shaw the pains of a victim of institutional power. And Cauchon, then, when his role is viewed on this inner stage, is not for Shaw what he in fact was—"a sadist, a bully, and a careerist who would stop at nothing," to use Bentley's words (461)—but rather an idealized, compromise figure, a man of compassion and reason who is nonetheless obliged to destroy life. Akin to "gentle Djerzinsky," Cauchon is for Shaw a gentle and reluctant agent of historical necessity, Shaw's ideal executioner. Shaw blocks his own recognition of Cauchon's disguised sadism because it might produce the shock of self-recognition.

These are the three figures—Joan, Stogumber, and Cauchon, who most serve as carriers of Shaw's emotions. Out of these divergent emotions, destructive as well as benign, out of a personal set of conflicts as much as out of the historical ones of the fifteenth century, Shaw was able to create in *Saint Joan* one of his most deeply felt and enduring masterpieces.

Epilogue

Saint Joan had a seriocomic real-life epilogue. It centered on a screenplay that Shaw completed in 1935. The prospective producer, Dr. Paul Czinner, submitted the script for comment to Catholic Action, an unofficial Vatican organization, and Monsignor M. Barbera, S.J. eventually replied from Rome that the film would not meet with any objections if it "appears to be according to the truth of the story and does not contain anything against the prestige of the Roman Catholic Church" (*CL*, 4:28). Father Barbera added, however, that the "mocking Irishman" had committed many violations of historical fact and would need to make revisions. The script was returned with suggested changes.

Shaw was outraged. He dispatched on 2 September 1936 a lengthy letter to the *New York Times* denouncing the attempt by a "Papal censor" to control his work. Even more incredible for him was the censor's failure to realize that his play thoroughly supported the Church. "*Saint Joan*," he stated,

> was hailed by all instructed Catholics as a very unexpected first installment of justice to the Church from Protestant quarters, and in effect, a vindication of the good faith of the famous trial at Rouen which had been held up to public execration for centuries as an abominable conspiracy, by a corrupt and treacherous Bishop of a villainous inquisition to murder an innocent girl.[1]

His play, he announced, will deepen the piety of any Catholic and will even make converts of Protestants. It presents "a perfectly legal trial in which the accused was, as far as the Church and the Holy Office were concerned, treated with special consideration and meticulous regard for the law." Joan had set up her own private judgment against the Church and claimed "that her conduct was a matter between God and herself. In this heresy she was adamant . . . [and] was beyond redemption. She had to face the stake and go through with it." Despite the Church's later condemning Cauchon for not permitting Joan to appeal to the Pope, "no appeal to the Pope could have saved her."

One can imagine the grounds for Shaw's outrage. Here was the one play of them all in which he had most curbed the "mocking Irishman" and reverently submitted himself to the saint's story. Here he had generously defended the fairness of the Church's trial of Joan and restored the integrity of the Inquisition and of a Bishop of the Church, Pierre Cauchon. In aiming at "the innermost attainable truth," he acknowledged that he had had to flatter Cauchon and whitewash him as much as the melodramatists had vilified and blackened him. He had also gone out of his way in his preface to honor the Church by saying there was absolutely no alternative to turning the relapsed heretic over to the secular authorities for burning. And now an ungrateful Vatican denounced his script, left him standing alone with his whitewash bucket, and called him a mere mocking Irishman.

It has the elements of a Shavian farce: Shaw the non-Christian strives to exculpate a Church that refuses to admit it was right and its Bishop honorable. Suddenly Shaw discovered that he had more reason than ever to sympathize with Joan: "Joan was sure she knew better than 'les gens de l'Eglise,' of whom apparently she had much the same opinion as I now have of the Catholic Action film censors." The man who annotated his script, he believed, was simply less familiar with Catholic dogma than he himself was,[2] and if Dr. Czinner had only "gone to the Pope he would have got his certificate and a blessing for me as well."[3] A minor official had blundered, the Pope would overrule him—Shaw, with unconscious irony, defended himself in the two ways he denied the Church the right to use in defending itself in regard to Joan's trial.

Who was right in this bizarre dispute? Clearly in his eagerness to have the Church accept his play as a gospel account of the events, Shaw neglected the consequences for the Church and for Joan. The Vatican would have to admit not only that the entire Rehabilitation proceedings of 1456 had been fraudulent, and its high officials accomplices in the fraud, but also that all the long years of its more recent deliberation had been wasted—the examining of the case in 1888, the formal proposal for canonization in 1903, the Beatification in 1909, the final canonization in 1920. Joan herself, then, was not a saint! For if, as Shaw declared, she truly was a heretic, an embryonic Protestant stubbornly maintaining that she would not "accept the church as the inspired interpreter of the will of God" but instead would trust to "her own private judgment" (as he says in his first letter), then she could not have been canonized. Shaw would save his play at the cost of Joan's sainthood!

The Church had slowly found a way, awkward and embarrassing as it was, to make amends. Millions of Catholics had welcomed the solemn canonization. And here was this nonbeliever, this Irish specialist in irreverent comedy, urging them in effect to reopen the investigation and change its conclusions to fit the much-disputed thesis of his play.

Under the circumstances, and given the strong criticisms Shaw had directed against the modern Church in his preface, the actual changes suggested by the Vatican annotator were remarkably moderate in number and tone, not at all indicating any desire to block the film. Most of them were valid corrections of historical errors, as when Shaw in his script has Joan placing the crown on Charles's head and the parenthetical emendation reads: "The Archbishop sits the crown on his head. Joan stands beside with the flag."[4] Or when the Archbishop of Rheims rebukes Charles's courtiers for laughing at him with the words "your mirth is a deadly sin," the emendation underlines "deadly sin" and marginally advises the use of "another word instead"—laughter not at all being such a sin. Several changes are protective of Joan only insofar as the remarks the dramatist gives her seem out of character and are not found in the records, as when on her first visit to the Dauphin she asks the Archbishop to send away all "these silly folk," and the Catholic reader underlines these improbable words; or when the script says "Joan's cannon fires another shot," and the reader rightly calls attention to an action that might imply she actually did battle rather than only carry the standard; or when she declares to the ecclesiastical court, "you are not fit that I should live among you," and the reader lines out the haughty, unhistorical words. Attention is called to Dunois's line "God is on the side of the big battalions," which would obviously not be said by a religious man. In short, most of the changes are such as would have been suggested by any friend of Shaw's with a close knowledge of the period.

There do remain, however, a handful of criticisms that seek to protect the Church even more than Joan, as when the Vatican reader writes "essentially damaging" next to the last scene's long passage in which the clerics debate whether to torture her and Canon Courcelles urges that it is always done. This suppresses the truth because Joan *was* shown instruments of torture to intimidate her and a vote was taken by 14 of the leading churchmen on whether to apply the instruments to her body. (The vote was 12 to 2 against it.) Again, the annotator at another point wants Joan to say she appeals to the Pope, for it is partly on Cauchon's blocking that appeal that the Church bases its case against him. Shaw omitted her requests that the case be brought to the Pope because he believed the Pope would simply have confirmed the verdict.

The Vatican annotator is very alert toward the end on the vexed question of whether Joan sought death to escape imprisonment and thus in a sense committed suicide. Had she committed that mortal sin, she could never have been canonized. (Shaw addresses this issue confusedly in his preface [21].) The annotator seeks to have the script avoid the issue by cutting mainly Joan's final speech—which Shaw had already halved in length—beginning "You think that life is nothing but not being stone dead," and going on to her declaration that she cannot live if cut off from "the wind in the trees, the larks in the sunshine, and the blessed, blessed church bells that send my angel voices floating to me on the wind."

This, of course, would seem to be an important deletion, but in fact Shaw should not have minded dropping the entire "liberty or death" speech since his first letter to the *Times* shows he had changed his mind. Joan, he now believes, knew she would still be a prisoner, but she wanted "to escape from the indecent custody of Warwick's soldiers into the custody of the church under conditions proper to her sex." Such imprisonment, he now maintains, was preferable to her than death.

All told, most of the suggested changes could readily have been made, and the others at least discussed, had the dramatist been interested in soothing the sensibilities of a powerful organization that had a right to advise the faithful if it deemed the film objectionable. But Shaw, who bristled at making cuts in *Saint Joan* at anyone's request (even the requests of friends like Lawrence Langner of New York's Theatre Guild, who rightly worried over the length), was scarcely one to heed the "papal censor" or any other censor. He would not betray the principles he had so eloquently defended in 1909 in the preface to *The Shewing-Up of Blanco Posnet.* Nevertheless, largely because of this refusal, the project languished and Shaw's screenplay was never produced.

A more rigorous Vatican reader could easily have found deeper heresies to protest. For as we saw earlier, Shaw shapes his play throughout to emphasize Joan's "Protestantism": her self-reliance and her right of private judgment against the Church. Shaw hardly attends to the virtues that contributed to her canonization—her charity to the poor, her kindliness, her constancy in taking the sacraments. For these he substitutes her ability to arouse the Dauphin and his soldiers to battle and her ability in the field. Her heroic virtues, as he represents them, are fundamentally secular. William Searle has cogently argued that the ideal of saintliness the play projects is anti-Catholic: it shows that man must be his own providence and that salvation lies in his own political keeping—he must save himself; it shows Joan more concerned with the state of the realm than with that of her soul; it shows that she is a saint because she is an enlightened heretic. And from all this Searle concludes that "in spite of Shaw's protestations to the contrary, *Saint Joan* is a profoundly anti-Catholic play" (113).

Must we conclude, then, that the Church was correct in contesting, even as mildly as it did, Shaw's view of the events? The answer is that both Shaw and the Church were probably right. The latter was accurate in concluding that the trial was unjust and Bishop Cauchon a prejudiced judge. But Shaw was right in concluding that the trial was "legal" and "very careful" and "exceptionally merciful in respect of sparing Joan the torture which was customary." Put the reverse way, Shaw was wrong in believing that the "conscientiousness" of the trial included any willingness to find Joan guiltless: the function of the trial was to prove her guilt to her, and that was achieved until she relapsed into heresy. And the Church was wrong in implying that Joan's trial was more significantly unfair, the priests who conducted it more biased, than at the trial of Jan Hus in 1415 or of Giordano Bruno in 1600, or at any of the thousands of other trials over several centuries for heresy and sorcery—ending in the victim's death by burning or hanging or torture—which finally made of the Inquisition an arm of the Church for which it must always ask forgiveness.

Happily, Christianity now seems to have matured to the point of no longer directly persecuting its heretics. But Shaw's great play can still serve to remind us of other trials behind legal facades in which the inquisitional spirit in more secular form still reigns, and in which the innocent and the idealistic, the unorthodox and possibly the truest benefactors of mankind can still be robbed of their lives.

Notes

Chapter 1

1. *Sixteen Self-Sketches* (New York: Dodd, Mead, 1949), 93.

2. Norman MacKensie and Jeanne MacKensie, *The Fabians* (New York: Simon & Schuster, 1977), 111.

3. Hesketh Pearson, *G. B. S.: A Full-Length Portrait* (New York: Harper, 1942), 293.

4. St. John Ervine, *Bernard Shaw: His Life. Work and Friends* (New York: William Morrow, 1956), 467; hereafter cited in text.

5. *The Matter with Ireland*, ed. David H. Greene and Dan H. Laurence (London: Rupert Hart-Davis, 1962), 113.

Chapter 2

1. T. F. Evans, ed., *Shaw: The Critical Heritage* (London: Routledge & Kegan Paul, 1976), 295; hereafter cited in text.

2. Daniel G. Gerould, "Saint Joan in Paris," *Shaw Review* 7 (January 1964); reprinted in *"Saint Joan" Fifty Years After*, ed. Stanley Weintraub (Baton Rouge: Louisiana State University Press, 1973), 217; hereafter cited in text.

Chapter 3

1. Desmond MacCarthy, *Shaw: The Plays* (Newton Abbot: David & Charles, 1973), 162; hereafter cited in text.

2. James Agate, *James Agate: An Anthology*, ed. Herbert Van Thal (New York: Hill & Wang, 1961), 69–70; hereafter cited in text.

3. Lawrence Langner, *G. B. S. and the Lunatic* (New York, Atheneum, 1963), 62.

4. Alice Griffin, "The New York Critics and Saint Joan," *Shaw Bulletin* 7 (January 1955): 11.

5. Irving McKee, "Shaw's *Saint Joan* and the American Critics," *Shavian* 2, no. 8 (February 1964): 15.

6. Brian Tyson, *The Story of Shaw's Saint Joan* (Kingston: McGill-Queens University Press, 1982), 86; hereafter cited in text.

7. The entire text of Pirandello's letter appears in the *New York Times*, 14 April 1924, section 8, p. 2.

8. James Graham, "Shaw on *Saint Joan*," *New York Times*, 13 April 1924, section 8, p. 2.

9. Kenneth Tynan, *Curtains* (New York: Atheneum, 1961), 83.

10. Martin Meisel, *Shaw and the Nineteenth-Century Theater* (Princeton: Princeton University Press, 1963), 365.

11. J. M. Robertson, *Mr. Shaw and "The Maid."* (London: Cobden-Sanderson, 1925); hereafter cited in text.

Chapter 4

1. The general shape of the play was not original. Shaw was familiar with Tom Taylor's 1871 *Jeanne Darc (Called the Maid)*, a five-act play in verse, largely based on the trial records as presented by Jules Quicherat. Taylor starts in Joan's village of Domremy, where Baudricourt visits her. There then are scenes in Chinon with the King, and scenes of Joan in full armor returning from battle. In act 4 the King is consecrated at Rheims, with Joan by his side. In act 5, in the torture chamber (which Shaw excludes), Joan abjures when she is shown the rack. She recants when she realizes she has denied her voices, not because she faces further imprisonment as in Shaw. Taylor's trial scene is much shorter than Shaw's. In sum, there are several similarities as well as many differences throughout. Shaw's version is far crisper and builds toward the elaborate trial scene. But Shaw may have borrowed a phrase for the famous last lines of his play from Taylor, who has Joan in the first act wondering when God will help further her mission and cries out: "How long, O Lord, how long?" (Tom Taylor, *Historical Dramas* [London: Chatto & Windus, 1877], 70). Shaw may also have been influenced to call his work "A Chronicle Play" by Taylor's similar designation. See also Meisel, 367–70.

2. "That's all flapdoodle up to there [end of scene 3]—just 'theatre' to get you interested—now the play begins." Remark by Shaw to Sybil Thorndike at a reading of the play; quoted in Raymond Mander and Joe Mitchenson, *Theatrical Companion to Shaw* (London: Rockliff, 1954), 14; hereafter cited in text.

3. Margery Morgan, *The Shavian Playground* (London: Methuen, 1972) 248–50.

4. BBC Broadcast Talk, 1931. Reprinted in *The Bodley Head Bernard Shaw: Collected Plays* (London: Max Reinhardt/Bodley Head, 1973), ed. Dan H. Laurence, 6:219; hereafter cited as Laurence.

Chapter 5

1. T. Douglas Murray, ed., *Jeanne D'Arc, Being the Story of her Life, her Achievements, and her Death, as attested on Oath and Set forth in the Original Documents* (London: William Heinemann, 1902), 80–81; hereafter cited in text as Murray.

2. Shaw thought of the chronicle play as one that stayed close to the historical documents yet told the story, as he said, "with an utter disregard

of the unity of place in a rapid succession of scenes" (quoted in Meisel, 365). The liberties Shaw took with the documents make doubtful the appropriateness of the term *chronicle*.

3. Sophocles, *Oedipus Rex* in *The Oedipus Cycle*, trans. Dudley Fitts and Robert Fitzgerald (New York: Harcourt, Brace, and World, 1949), 44.

4. William Searle, *The Saint and the Skeptics* (Detroit: Wayne State University Press, 1976), 116; hereafter cited in text.

5. Louis Crompton, *Shaw the Dramatist* (Lincoln: University of Nebraska Press, 1969), 207.

6. *Bernard Shaw: Collected Letters*, ed. Dan H. Laurence (New York: Viking Penguin, 1985, 1988), 3:554; hereafter cited in text as *CL*.

Chapter 7

1. Daniel Rankin and Claire Quintal, eds., *The First Biography of Joan of Arc* (Pittsburgh: University of Pittsburgh Press, 1964), 45; hereafter cited in text.

2. Raphael Holinshed, *Chronicles of England, Scotland and Ireland* (London: J. Johnsons, 1808), 3:171–72.

Chapter 8

1. Edmund Wilson, "Bernard Shaw Since the War," *New Republic*, 27 August 1924, 381.

2. A. N. Kaul, *The Action of English Comedy* (New Haven: Yale University Press, 1970), 324.

3. Holly Hill, ed., *Playing Joan: Actresses on the Challenge of Shaw's Saint Joan* (New York: Theatre Communications Group, 1977), 76; hereafter cited in text as Hill.

4. Maurice Valency, *The Cart and the Trumpet* (New York: Oxford University Press, 1973), 388; hereafter cited in text.

5. Nicholas Grene, *Bernard Shaw: A Critical View* (New York: St. Martin's Press, 1984), 147.

Chapter 9

1. Johan Huizinga, "Bernard Shaw's Saint," in *Men and Ideas* (New York: Meridian, 1959), 219; hereafter cited in text.

2. J. Van Kan, "Bernard Shaw's Saint Joan: An Historical Point of View," *Fortnightly Review* 118 (July 1925): 42; hereafter cited in text.

3. Ingvald Raknem, *Joan of Arc: In History, Legend and Literature* (Oslo: Universitetsforlaget, 1971), 195–96; hereafter cited in text.

4. Stanley Weintraub, "Bernard Shaw's Other Saint Joan," *South Atlantic Quarterly* (Spring 1965), reprinted in Weintraub, ed., *Saint Joan Fifty Years After*, 233. It is difficult to understand how Weintraub missed the obvious and decisive contrasts between the characters of Joan and T. E. Lawrence, contrasts that Shaw would easily have recognized. Unlike Joan, Lawrence as an adult was not religious; unlike her, he was naturally shy and self-deprecating, aloof, learned, self-conscious, secretive—"a troubled

creature, a rich mind in a hurt body," as a fellow airman, G. W. Dunn, described him (A. W. Lawrence, ed., *T. E. Lawrence by His Friends* [New York: Doubleday, Doran 1937], 399). Even physically, the two individuals were contrasting, Joan being of sturdy build and strength whereas Lawrence was of "short and slight body" (389).

Weintraub's reasoning is very odd. He claims that Joan, like Lawrence, was short and laconic (234), but there is no evidence that such descriptions fit Joan at all. Nor is there any evidence to support Weintraub's notion that Joan would have retreated to a convent (235); on the contrary, the Count de Dunois heard her express the desire to return to the family farm (Murray, 240–41). Nor can an anecdote Shaw told *omitting* mention of Lawrence serve as evidence (as Weintraub claims [236]) that Shaw associated Lawrence with Joan. Weintraub insists that Shaw wrote the play with Lawrence's *Seven Pillars of Wisdom* "at his elbow" (231, 233), that is, on the desk of his country home, yet in fact Shaw wrote much of the play in Ireland. Weintraub's case is further undermined by his claim elsewhere to have spotted Lawrence as the model for two markedly different characters in a later Shaw play (*Too True to Be Good*), yet neither of these supposed Lawrencian figures at all resembles Joan (*Shaw Review* 7 [May 1964]: 54–57).

Weintraub's unreliability and poor judgment here are characteristic of his other writings on Shaw and may be partly what the distinguished English critic Geoffrey Grigson had in mind when he called Weintraub a barbarous writer (*New York Review of Books*, 26 January 1978, 36).

5. *Pierre Champion*, "On the Trial of Jeanne d'Arc," in *The Trial of Jeanne d'Arc*, ed. W. P. Barrett, (New York: Gotham House, 1932), 480, 498; hereafter cited in text as Champion.

6. Victoria Sackville-West, *Saint Joan of Arc* (Boston: G. K. Hall, 1984), 274.

7. Henri Guillemin, *Joan, Maid of Orléans* (New York: Saturday Review Press, 1973), 177.

8. A. M. Cohen, "The 'Shavianization' of Cauchon," *Shaw Review* 20, no. 2 (May 1977): 68.

9. The behavior of the Church within Charles's realm, after Joan's victory at Orléans, is fairly described by Charles in Shakespeare's *Henry VI, Part I*:

> 'Tis Joan, not we, by whom the day is won;
> For which I will divide by crown with her,
> And all the priests and friars in my realm
> Shall in procession sing her endless praise. (1.6., 17–20)

10. Cauchon's refusal to accept Joan's appeal to the Pope is odd, since the Pope would probably have sustained the verdict. The position of the papacy, after a century of troubles and the great schism, was extremely weak; and the new Pope, Eugene IV, with the Council of Basle looming, would have been unlikely to oppose the powerful University of Paris, which had

vehemently condemned Joan. But perhaps Cauchon, apprehensive that Charles VII would somehow exert influence on the Holy See, determined not to risk any modification of the verdict. Cauchon's decision later proved convenient to the Church, which was able to claim in the Rehabilitation proceedings that the blocked papal appeal contributed to the trial's illegality.

Chapter 10

1. William Butler Yeats, "The Circus Animals' Desertion," *Collected Poems* (London: Macmillan, 1961), 392.

2. Preface to *On the Rocks*, in *Prefaces by Bernard Shaw* (London: Odhams, 1938), 353; the volume is hereafter cited in text as *Prefaces*.

3. Bernard Shaw, "On Ritual, Religion, and the Intolerableness of Tolerance," in *Shaw on Religion*, ed. Warren Sylvester Smith (London: Constable, 1967), 148–171; hereafter cited in text as Smith.

4. Eric Bentley, *What Is Theatre* (New York: Atheneum, 1968), 256; hereafter cited in text.

5. *The Rationalization of Russia*, ed. Harry M. Geduld (Bloomington: Indiana University Press, 1964), 73; hereafter cited in text.

6. Bernard Shaw, *Everybody's Political What's What?* (New York: Dodd, Mead, 1944), 282, 283.

7. Arnold Silver, *Bernard Shaw: The Darker Side* (Stanford: Stanford University Press, 1982), chapters 2 and 5, and afterword.

8. Richard Nickson doubtless earns the palm as the most bemused of Shaw's idolaters. In a series of articles he has sought to obfuscate Shaw's well-known support for such dictators as Mussolini, Hitler, and Stalin. See "G. B. S.: British Fascist?" *Shavian*, October 1959, reprinted in *Independent Shavian* 16, nos. 2–3; "Was Shaw a Mosleyite?" *Shavian*, September 1960, reprinted in *Independent Shavian* 17, nos. 1–2; "Shaw and the Dictators," *Independent Shavian* 18, no. 1. What Geoffrey Allen wrote of Nickson's first article unfortunately applies to them all: "Dr. Richard Nickson is a little too slaphappy with his whitewash brush in his rebuttal . . . of those who charged Shaw with flirting with Fascism." (*Shavian*, February 1960). Nickson's continued slaphappy exercise of his brush has regrettably, if justly, been dubbed the Richard Nickson cover-up. For an accurate account of Shaw's views, see his friend St. John Ervine's biography of him, Allan Chappelow's *Shaw—The Chucker-Out* (London: George Allen & Unwin, 1969), or Arland Ussher's *Three Great Irishmen* (New York: Devin-Adair, 1953).

Epilogue

1. *New York Times*, 14 September 1936, 26.

2. *New York Times*, 17 September 1936, 18.

3. *New York Times*, 27 September 1936, 14N.

4. All emendations are drawn from appendix B of *Saint Joan: A Screenplay by Bernard Shaw*, ed. Bernard F. Dukore (Seattle: University of Washington Press, 1968), 143–47.

Selected Bibliography

PRIMARY SOURCES

Bernard Shaw: Collected Letters. Edited by Dan H. Laurence. Vols. 3–4. New York: Viking Penguin, 1985, 1988.

Everybody's Political What's What? New York: Dodd, Mead, 1944.

The Prefaces. London: Odhams Press, 1938.

The Rationalization of Russia. Edited by Harry M. Geduld. Bloomington: Indiana University Press, 1964.

Saint Joan. Vol. 6 of *The Bodley Head Bernard Shaw.* London: Max Reinhardt/The Bodley Head, 1973.

Saint Joan. Vol. 17 of *The Collected Works of Bernard Shaw.* Ayot St. Lawrence Edition. New York: William H. Wise, 1930.

Saint Joan: A Screenplay by Bernard Shaw. Edited by Barnard F. Dukore. Seattle: University of Washington Press, 1968.

Shaw: An Autobiography. Edited by Stanley Weintraub. 2 vols. New York: Weybright & Talley, 1969, 1970.

Shaw on Religion. Edited by Warren Sylvester Smith. London: Constable, 1967.

SECONDARY SOURCES

Biographies

Chappelow, Allan. *Shaw—"The Chucker-Out."* London: Allen & Unwin, 1969.

Ervine, St. John. *Bernard Shaw.* New York: William Morrow, 1956.

Holroyd, Michael. *Bernard Shaw.* 3 vols. New York: Random House, 1988, 1989, 1991.

Pearson, Hesketh. *G. B. S.: A Full-Length Portrait.* New York: Harper, 1942.

Books on "Saint Joan"

Bloom, Harold, ed. *George Bernard Shaw's "Saint Joan": A Collection of Critical Essays.* New York: Chelsea House, 1987. A convenient collection of articles and of relevant chapters from several leading Shaw studies, including work by Berst, Crompton, Grene, Martz, Morgan, and Searle.

Hill, Holly, ed. *Playing Joan: Actresses on the Challenge of Shaw's "Saint Joan".* New York: Theatre Communications Group, 1987. Fresh perspectives on aspects of the work from the player's standpoint.

Margolis, Nadia. *Joan of Arc in History, Literature, and Film: A Critical Bibliography.* New York: Garland, 1990. Well-annotated and extensive coverage, with a discerning essay.

Mason, W. H. *St. Joan.* Oxford: Blackwell, 1964. An astute scene-by-scene analysis but without comment on the play's historicity.

Robertson, J. M. *Mr. Shaw and "The Maid."* London: Cobden-Sanderson, 1925. A provocative rationalist polemic that acknowledges the brilliance of the play but attacks its historicity and the preface's accuracy.

Tyson, Brian. *The Story of Shaw's "Saint Joan."* Kingston: McGill-Queens University Press, 1982. Primarily a scene-by-scene study of Shaw's first draft and its subsequent revisions—much interesting material though too uniformly adulatory.

Weintraub, Stanley, ed. *"Saint Joan" Fifty Years After.* Baton Rouge: Louisiana State University Press, 1973. A useful collection of articles and chapters from books, including among other writers Pirandello, Huizinga, Robertson, T. S. Eliot, Martz, Gerould, and Kaul.

Books with Sections on "Saint Joan"

Bentley, Eric. *Bernard Shaw.* Norfolk: New Directions, 1947. A perceptive short defense of Shaw as dramatist and thinker.

Berst, Charles. *Bernard Shaw and the Art of Drama.* Urbana: University of Illinois Press, 1973. The play viewed as spiritual epic and tragicomedy, "qualifying the supernatural with the human" and linking "the human to great abstractions."

Crompton, Louis. *Shaw the Dramatist.* Lincoln: University of Nebraska Press, 1969. A judicious and influential exploration of the play as an anti-Aristotelian, Hegelian tragedy, indicating Shaw's hostility to Renaissance ethics and aesthetics.

Dukore, Bernard. *Bernard Shaw, Playwright: Aspects of Shavian Drama.* Columbia: University of Missouri Press, 1973. An eccentric but often suggestive study.

Evans, T. F. *Shaw: The Critical Heritage.* London: Routledge & Kegan Paul, 1976. Fourteen reviews and comments on the play, including work by Pirandello, Agate, and T. S. Eliot.

Grene, Nicholas. *Bernard Shaw: A Critical View.* New York: St. Martin's, 1984. An appreciative and occasionally discriminating essay on the play.

Huizinga, Johan. *Men and Ideas.* New York: Meridian, 1959. In the chapter "Bernard Shaw's Saint," this leading medieval historian finds both fidelities and inaccuracies in Shaw's depiction of Joan and her age.

Kaul, A. N. *The Action of English Comedy.* New Haven: Yale University Press, 1970. Contains a stimulating chapter on Shaw's dramas with incisive comments on *Saint Joan.*

Langner, Lawrence. *G. B. S. and the Lunatic.* New York: Atheneum, 1963. A behind-the-scenes look at the negotiations for the first production of the play and Langner's futile efforts to have the dramatist shorten it.

MacCarthy, Desmond. *Shaw: The Plays.* Newton Abbot: David & Charles, 1973. Includes three acute reviews of *Saint Joan* by a wise contemporary critic.

Mayer, Hans. *Outsiders.* Cambridge: MIT Press, 1984. The chapter "The Scandal of Joan of Arc: Schiller, Shaw, Brecht, Vishnevskii" gives Shaw's version a high comparative rating.

Meisel, Martin. *Shaw and the Nineteenth-Century Theater.* Princeton: Princeton University Press, 1963. A painstaking study of Shaw's indebtedness to earlier theatrical works and traditions, with *Saint Joan* seen as a direct descendant of "the heroic history play written for a woman star."

Morgan, Margery. *The Shavian Playground.* London: Methuen, 1972. Concentrates on the work as incorporating the traditions of the passion play and the pantomime.

Raknem, Ingvald. *Joan of Arc: In History, Legend, and Literature.* Oslo: Universitetsforlaget, 1971. An erudite survey of its subject, with a highly critical view of Shaw's misrepresentations of history and of the character of Joan.

Searle, William. *The Saint and the Skeptics: Joan of Arc in the Work of Mark Twain, Anatole France, and Bernard Shaw.* Detroit: Wayne State University Press, 1976. A powerful essay presenting Joan as an exponent of Shaw's philosophy and the play as anti-Catholic.

Stewart, J. I. M. *Eight Modern Writers.* Oxford: Oxford University Press, 1963. After a long chapter on Shaw, the critic finds that *Saint Joan* is his finest play, with Joan his most truly human being.

Valency, Maurice. *The Cart and the Trumpet: The Plays of George Bernard Shaw.* New York: Oxford University Press, 1973. Urbane reflections on the distinctiveness of the play by an eminent historian of modern drama.

Wisenthal, J. M. *The Marriage of Contraries: Bernard Shaw's Middle Plays.* Cambridge: Harvard University Press, 1974. A wide-ranging discussion relating Shaw's outlook in the play and his characterization of Joan to his general philosophy.

_____. *Shaw's Sense of History.* Oxford: Clarendon Press, 1988. Considers how "some of the dramatic strength of *Saint Joan* derives from the collision in Shaw's own mind between the Feudal, Catholic values of the Middle Ages and the Capitalist, Protestant values of the Renaissance."

Articles on "Saint Joan"

Austin, Don. "Comedy through Tragedy: Dramatic Structure in *Saint Joan.*" *Shaw Review* 8 (1965): 52–62. Claims that the play has a comic tone, with the epilogue providing a happy ending.

Barnet, Sylvan. "Bernard Shaw on Tragedy." *PMLA* 71 (1956): 888–99. Reviews Shaw's distaste for the finality of tragic drama and maintains that, for Shaw, Joan was not a tragic hero, since she accomplished her mission and was later canonized.

Boas, Frederick S. "Joan of Arc in Shakespeare, Schiller and Shaw." *Shakespeare Quarterly* 2 (1951): 35–45. A summary of the three contrasting characterizations, with measured praise for Shakespeare's usually disparaged portrait.

Cohen, A. M. "The 'Shavianization' of Cauchon." *Shaw Review* 20, no. 2 (1977): 63–70. Ably examines Shaw's whitewashing of Bishop Cauchon and speculates on the playwright's motives for doing so.

Fielden, John. "Shaw's *Saint Joan* as Tragedy." *Twentieth Century Literature* 3 (1957): 59–67. Maintains that the play is akin to classical tragedy in that "a good person falls to death because of pride and a tragic error."

Gerould, Daniel C. "*Saint Joan* in Paris." *Shaw Review* 7 (1964): 11–23. Informative analysis of positive French reaction to an outsider's play on their national heroine.

Griffin, Alice. "The New York Critics and *Saint Joan.*" *Shaw Bulletin* 1 (1965): 10–15. Recounts the mixed first reactions to the play's premiere.

Martz, Louis. "The Saint as Tragic Hero: *Saint Joan* and *Murder in the Cathedral.*" In *Tragic Themes in Western Literature*, edited by Cleanth Brooks. New Haven: Yale University Press, 1955. Reprinted in Bloom and in Weintraub collections (see above). Compares the two works and concludes that although Shaw's play has a tragic tension, Joan is not a truly flawed Aristotelian tragic hero.

Riggs, Lawrason. "Joan of Arc—Heretic or Saint?" *Commonweal*, 2 November 1934, 16–18. Disputes Shaw's contention that the original (1431) trial was fair and the Rehabilitation process (1456) fraudulent.

Solomon, Stanley. "Saint Joan as Epic Tragedy." *Modern Drama* 6 (February 1964): 437–49. Discusses the play as a special kind of tragedy, its anticipatory scenes coordinating epic and tragic elements.

Stoppel, Hans. "Shaw and Sainthood." *English Studies* 36 (1955): 49–63. See Joan as the best representative of a later, more spiritualized Shavian ideal type, differing from such earlier heroes as Caesar and Tanner.

Van Kan, J. "Bernard Shaw's Saint Joan: An Historical Point of View." *Fortnightly Review* 118 (July 1925): 36–46. A historian's appreciative reaction to the play, but with significant reservations about its accuracy regarding King Charles and Joan.

Selected Bibliography

Books on the Historical Saint Joan

Barrett, W. P., ed. *The Trial of Jeanne d'Arc.* New York: Gotham House, 1932. Contains documents from the trial as well as an essay by Pierre Champion.

Fabre, Lucien. *Joan of Arc.* London: Odhams Press, 1954.

France, Anatole. *The Life of Joan of Arc.* New York: Dodd, Mead, 1923.

Guillemin, Henri. *Joan, Maid of Orléans.* New York: Saturday Review Press, 1973.

Lucie-Smith, Edward. *Joan of Arc.* New York: W. W. Norton, 1976.

Murray, T. Douglas, ed. *Jeanne D'Arc, Being the Story of her Life, her Achievements, and her Death, as attested on Oath and Set forth in the Original Documents.* London: William Heinemann, 1902.

Pernoud, Regine. *Joan of Arc.* Harmondsworth: Penguin Books, 1969.

Rankin, Daniel, and Claire Quintal, eds. *The First Biography of Joan of Arc.* Pittsburgh: University of Pittsburgh Press, 1964.

Sackville-West, Victoria. *Saint Joan of Arc.* Boston: G. K. Hall, 1984.

Other Plays on Saint Joan

Anderson, Maxwell. *Joan of Lorraine.* Washington, D.C.: Anderson House, 1946.

Anouilh, Jean. *The Lark.* New York: Random House, 1956.

Mackaye, Percy. *Jeanne d'Arc.* New York: Macmillan, 1906.

Péguy, Charles. *Mystery of the Charity of Joan of Arc.* Translated by Julian Green. London: Hollis and Carter, 1950.

Schiller, Friedrich. *Die Jungfrau von Orléans (The Maiden of Orléans).*

Shakespeare, William. *Henry VI, Part I.*

Taylor, Tom. *Jeanne Darc.* In *Historical Dramas.* London: Chatto & Windus, 1877.

Index

The Author

Arnold Silver is a professor of English at the University of Massachusetts at Amherst. He is the author of *Bernard Shaw: The Darker Side* (1982) and the editor of *The Family Letters of Samuel Butler* (1962). He is coinventor of a political game called Credibility Gap, and has written children's stories and an off-Broadway play entitled *Crisis in Hell*.